Supporting Indigenous Children's Development

Supporting Indigenous Children's Development

COMMUNITY-UNIVERSITY PARTNERSHIPS

Jessica Ball and Alan Pence

UBCPress · Vancouver · Toronto

Library and Archives Canada Cataloguing in Publication

Ball, Jessica, 1952-
    Supporting Indigenous children's development : community-university partnerships / Jessica Ball and Alan Pence.

Includes bibliographical references and index.
ISBN-13: 978-0-7748-1230-6
ISBN-10: 0-7748-1230-3

    1. Indian children – Education (Preschool) – Canada. 2. Indian children – Care – Canada. 3. Community education – Canada. 4. Early childhood education – Curricula – Canada. 5. Early childhood teachers – Training of – Canada. 6. Community and college – Canada. I. Pence, Alan R., 1948- II. Title.

E96.2.B35 2006   372.21089'97071   C2006-905005-8

Canadä

UBC Press gratefully acknowledges the financial support for our publishing program of the Government of Canada through the Book Publishing Industry Development Program (BPIDP), and of the Canada Council for the Arts, and the British Columbia Arts Council.

This book has been published with the help of a grant from the Canadian Federation for the Humanities and Social Sciences, through the Aid to Scholarly Publications Programme, using funds provided by the Social Sciences and Humanities Research Council of Canada.

UBC Press
The University of British Columbia
2029 West Mall
Vancouver, BC V6T 1Z2
604-822-5959 / Fax: 604-822-6083
www.ubcpress.ca

Contents

Preface

This book describes the evolution and practice of an innovative community-based partnership approach to strengthening community capacity to design, deliver, and evaluate culturally appropriate programs to support young children's development. The approach, created through partnerships between First Nations in Canada and the authors at the University of Victoria, represents a significant departure from the established and familiar paths of training and education in North America, which typically promote knowledge transmission and prescribed best practices based on assumptions of their universal validity and desirability. The success of this partnership approach has meant stepping outside expected institutional relationships to identify a common ground of caring, respect, and flexibility, and an orientation toward action from which collaboration in program delivery and co-construction of curriculum can flow.

The pilot partnership that led to the First Nations Partnership Programs was initiated in 1989 by Meadow Lake Tribal Council, representing nine Cree and Dene First Nations in the province of Saskatchewan in north-central Canada. The Tribal Council had determined that the future well-being of these communities rested on the current health and wellness of their children. Since its formation in the early 1980s, Meadow Lake Tribal Council had undertaken several training and economic development ventures. Without reliable child care services, however, participants in the training programs were often forced to drop out. Small business developments, many of which depended on single parents as entrepreneurs and employees, were struggling (Pence and McCallum 1994). The Tribal Council's constituent communities recognized an urgent need for child care services "developed, administered, and operated by [our] own people" (Meadow Lake Tribal Council 1989). The communities wanted to ensure that child care services reflected community knowledge, culture, and values.

Meadow Lake Tribal Council developed a long-range plan to educate community members in early childhood care and development (ECCD). It envisioned that these practitioners would "walk in both worlds" (Louis Opikokew, tribal Elder coordinator) – the world of non-Indigenous, largely urban-based ECCD and the world of the nine rural Cree and Dene communities represented by the Tribal Council. This vision was the starting point for an innovative approach to co-constructing a bicultural university diploma program in child and youth care focusing on early childhood. The approach has evolved continuously through ten diploma deliveries (ten partnerships) with nine tribal organizations and Indigenous child and family service agencies. These bicultural partnerships have come to be known collectively as the First Nations Partnership Programs. More than sixty First Nations communities in rural areas of western Canada have been involved. Although distributed across distances up to twenty-five hundred kilometres and applied in very different cultural and institutional contexts, the First Nations Partnership Programs, with their partnership approach, have thrived. The programs have had immediate positive impact on caregiving and the development of services for children, as well as far-reaching impacts on community capacity, empowerment, and revitalization of cultural and social structures. The words of some of the partners in the journey described in this book convey their excitement in co-creating an effective approach to strengthening capacity for Indigenous early childhood programs:

> It has been sixteen years since our initial contact with the School of Child and Youth Care, University of Victoria, in 1989. Our dream was to develop early childhood training for First Nation child care workers. Our thoughts at the time were of readiness toward development and operation of First Nation child care facilities on reserve. Who would have thought that the spin-offs to community pride, community development, community empowerment, care and safety of children, community awareness of early childhood development, identity of community strengths and integration and development of many more program initiatives which support children and families would be the outcomes of this initial work? (Marie McCallum, administrator, Meadow Lake Tribal Council)

I think what this program has is truly bicultural, where they have the Indigenous philosophy being the core of the program, being the first priority in the whole two-year curriculum. They also have the same academic excellence ... It's not that the program gives them that Indigenous way, they've had it, they know it, and the process just allows it to come out ... Students say, "Our story is important." "Listen to my story." They become convinced that their cultural history and experience are important. (Lisa Sterling, instructor, Nzen'man' Child and Family Services)

We are working hard in Lil'wat Nation to develop our human resources and to create strong programs, and I think that having the interest from the university in what we're doing here is very positive. It holds a mirror up for everyone to see what we're doing, and it amplifies the excitement.

We want to retain the staff we have helped to develop, and keep qualified people working in our community, and so for them to hear from researchers that other people are interested in what is going on here, and that we are doing things here that can be useful for others to learn from, that's good ... And especially in the way that the research is being done – developing long-term relationships, making sure everyone knows what they are agreeing to, and ensuring benefit to the community itself ... there is a mutuality and respect that I think is exemplary. (Sheldon Tetreault, senior administrator, Lil'wat Nation)

The training in early childhood care and development brought forth more programs – not only child care – but [other programs] for children and families. This is still growing. Two of the First Nations just started a child care and development program – expanded beyond the Aboriginal Head Start program. They are sharing, and this sharing is also an outcome of the communication and understanding that developed between people who were originally students in the post-secondary training together. It is good to see the communities working together in this way. (Diane Bigfoot, education coordinator, Treaty 8 Tribal Association)

After participating in ten partnership programs with First Nations, we are convinced that the popular demand for culturally sensitive programs cannot be met through established education and professionalization practices. To respond meaningfully to the goals and practices of cultural communities – and to the children and families within them – we must acknowledge the cultural specificity of mainstream research, theory, and professional practice and forge new understandings for preparing human service practitioners to work in cultural communities. By telling the story of the First Nations Partnership Programs, we hope to encourage and support the elaboration and extension of an alternative discourse to the largely exclusionary, Western, modernist agenda of ECCD, which defines universal care principles and best practices to the neglect of many good ways and a multitude of good practices.

Acknowledgments

Over the course of seventeen years and ten partnership programs, we have been privileged to have been invited by nine groups of First Nations in western Canada to visit and work in their traditional territories. We have been welcomed as partners, colleagues, and friends. It has been an honour to have shared with these partners the journey of these explorations in the space between our cultures.

Writing the story of our journey with First Nations in the partnership programs has been a joint effort, and authorship is listed alphabetically. Alan Pence initiated the First Nations Partnership Programs in 1989 through the partnership with the Meadow Lake Tribal Council, and coordinated partnerships with four other communities through 1998. Jessica Ball joined Alan in 1996, and in 1998 she became the coordinator of program deliveries with the five most recent groups of community partners. She also undertook the main program evaluation and related research studies.

A program like the First Nations Partnership Program could not succeed without a community of diversely talented people committed to nation rebuilding and children's well-being. These people worked in First Nations communities and university offices. They were variously engaged as Elders sharing their cultural knowledge and wisdom, as content specialists and advisors, as donors, institutional administrators, instructors, and student counsellors. While space does not allow for the identification of all who played important roles, we would like to recognize a number of key contributors.

In the earliest days of the First Nations Partnership Program (even before it had that name), Ray Ahenakew, Vern Bachiu, Mary Rose Opekokew, Marie McCallum, Louis Opikokew, Chief Richard Gladue, Frieda Iron, and

Brian Opikokew, all associated with the Meadow Lake Tribal Council, ensured that the program had a solid start. At the University of Victoria, Lynette Jackson (Halldorson), Margo Greenwood, and Betty Cameron were indispensable. The insights of Drs. Betty Jones, Emmy Werner, Don Barr, and Cassie Landers helped identify principles that would guide the program over time. A formative evaluation by Elder Debbie Jette yielded insights that were invaluable for understanding the program as not just education but as an educational approach to culturally appropriate community development.

The second partnership – with the Cowichan Tribes of Vancouver Island and the Cowichan Campus of Malaspina University-College – became the first three-way partnership delivery. Louise Underwood, Carol Matthews, Ruth Kroek, Diana Elliott, Sharon Tilly, Linda McDonell, and Lynn Trainor all supported the program's development in this new context.

Several partnerships commenced in the mid-1990s involving Treaty 8 Tribal Association (northeast British Columbia), Tl'azt'en Nation (north-central British Columbia), Lil'wat Nation (southwest British Columbia), Nzen'man' Child and Family Services (Fraser Canyon), and Onion Lake First Nation (Saskatchewan). The partnership with Onion Lake First Nation brought in a second institutional partner, the Saskatchewan Indian Institute of Technologies (SIIT). Key persons involved in those partnerships include Diane Bigfoot, Chief Judy Maas, and Bev Wice with Treaty 8; Amelia Stark, Liz Burtch, Ginny Henniger, and Leisa Rossum with Tl'azt'en Nation; Christine Leo, Verna Stager, Jeanette Joe, Felicity Nelson, and Martina Pierre with Lil'wat Nation; Romona Baxter, Lisa Sterling, and Lana Maki with Nzen'man' Child and Family Services; Jenny Whitstone, Margaret Mulbach, Joanne McDonald, Brian MacDonald, and Terry Clark with Onion Lake First Nation; and Guy Poncelet and Dennis Esperanz with SIIT.

Since 2000, the program has been delivered twice through partnerships with the Little Shuswap Indian Band (central British Columbia), involving Chief Felix Arnouse, Joan Arnouse, Wes François, Brenda Robinson, and key instructors Kathy Leonhardt, Sandy Burgess, and Laura Jamieson. At the time of this writing, the First Nations Partnership Program is engaged in a thriving partnership with Penelakut Tribe (Kuper Island, British Columbia), involving six First Nations in central Vancouver Island, with support from band manager Lisa Shaver and education coordinator Cecilia Harris and teachings by Elder Florence James and instructor Heather Joe. In addition, both Malaspina University-College and SIIT continue to offer the program with First Nations partners in British Columbia and Saskatchewan.

The university-based team has benefited from the contributions of several talented curriculum writers as the courses have been developed, expanded, and updated over many years. Debts of gratitude are owed especially to Vicki Mulligan, Heather Siska, Susan Gage, Robin Hood, Carol Orom, Silvia Vilches, Enid Elliot, and Arlene Wells. Onowa McIvor and Silvia Vilches served capably in community liaison and many other roles over several years. Both completed masters' degrees while employed with the program and have gone on to pursue their doctorates. We also wish to thank support staff members, including Vicky Point, Lori Isaac, Rena Conibear, Karen Fitzgerald, Corrine Lowen, and Jaime Apolonio.

The partnering First Nations communities secured their own funds to prepare for and deliver the program. Several communities worked for many years to secure funds from combinations of federal, provincial, and local and regional sources. The curriculum was developed, revised, and extended over the years with the help of the Child Care Initiatives Fund of Human Resources Development Canada and the Vancouver Foundation. The Lawson Foundation and the Vancouver Foundation funded the production of a set of video documentaries requested by First Nations partners to share the excitement of their innovations in initiating university-accredited training partnerships. The program evaluation research and a longitudinal follow-up study of graduates' careers and community-based program development were funded primarily by the Child Care Visions Social Development Partnerships Program of Human Resources Development Canada.

The First Nations Partnership Programs have enjoyed strong support from the directors of the University of Victoria's School of Child and Youth Care, Drs. Jim Anglin, Valerie Kuehne, and Sibylle Artz, as well as from the deans of the Faculty of Human and Social Development at the University of Victoria. Allison Benner deserves our deepest gratitude for her thoughtful and informed contributions to the articulation of ideas in the preparation of this book. We thank Leslie Prpich for her careful editorial work on the manuscript.

No sustained social development initiative occurs in isolation. Communities do matter, and we feel honoured and blessed to have been joined by so many talented and caring people dedicated to preserving cultural diversity and sustaining richly encultured communities for children to belong to, develop, and co-create.

Supporting Indigenous Children's Development

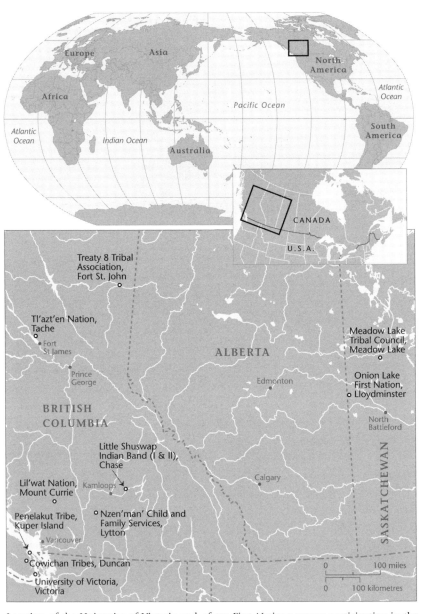

Location of the University of Victoria and of ten First Nations groups participating in the partnership program

Turning the World Upside Down

It will be children who inherit the struggle to retain and enhance the people's culture, language and history, who continue the quest for economic progress for a better quality of life, and who move forward with a strengthened resolve to plan their own destiny.

– Meadow Lake Tribal Council (1989)

First Nations' Priorities for Children

Over one million people in Canada identify as Aboriginal, including approximately 700,000 First Nations, 70,000 Inuit, and 260,000 Métis peoples (Statistics Canada 2001b). First Nations are culturally and linguistically diverse, comprising eleven distinct language groups (Statistics Canada 2001a). About half of the First Nations population lives on lands reserved for them by the federal government;[1] among the half that resides off reserves, most live in urban centres (Statistics Canada 2001b).

The Indigenous population is young, with a mean age of 25.5 years – ten years younger than that of the non-Indigenous population – and its birth rate is almost double that of other populations in Canada (Statistics Canada 2001b).[2] The Assembly of First Nations, representing First Nations in Canada living on federal reserve lands, has urged that caregivers be trained

---

1 Groups of First Nations on reserves are often organized for administrative purposes into tribal councils or tribal associations representing several communities that are usually clustered together geographically. Constituent communities may or may not share the same cultural and migration history, language, and customs.

2 The terms "Indigenous" and "Aboriginal" refer to the same groupings of peoples who identify themselves as descendants of original habitants of the land that is now called

in communities to support the burgeoning population of First Nations children needing comprehensive care in a culturally appropriate manner (1989, Recommendation 39). The need for child care facilities and trained community members to staff them is particularly urgent for families living on federal reserve lands, where access to child care, health, and development services is limited by geographic distances, social and cultural barriers, and eligibility regulations.

Many First Nations are prioritizing early childhood care and development (ECCD) training and services as a prerequisite for economic development and as a way to protect and enhance the physical and psychosocial health and the cultural identities of First Nations children and families. Like many Indigenous groups around the globe, First Nations in Canada are seeking ways to ensure the survival, or revival, of their cultural beliefs, values, and practices, while at the same time wanting to ensure that their community members have access to and competence in the dominant society (Armstrong, Kennedy, and Oberle 1990; Battiste 2000; Le Roux 1999; Smith, Burke, and Ward 2000).

As First Nations exercise greater political control over their futures, they are understandably wary of so-called best practices and improvements from the dominant society (Battiste 2000). First Nations peoples in Canada have been subject to every kind of colonial assault, from assimilationist requirements to genocidal practices (Barman 1996; Greenwood and Fraser 2005; McMillan 1995; Ross 1992). Reams of poignant testimony describe the suffering caused by the infliction of Western best practices – including enforced residential schooling, child welfare practices that undermine extended family support systems, and other "helping" services – all deemed at the time to be in the best interests of Aboriginal children and their families (Fournier and Crey 1997; Haig-Brown 1988; Ing 2000; Lederman 1999; Waldram 2004; White and Maxim 2003; White, Maxim, and Beavon 2004).

First Nations communities in rural areas perceive a disconnection between mainstream ECCD training programs and their own distinct circumstances, histories, cultures, and goals. In most universities and colleges, theories and methods of ECCD are grounded in largely Euro-North American developmental theory and research, and are often seen by First Nations

---

Canada. Some of these people prefer the term "Indigenous" because it connects them to a global advocacy movement of Indigenous peoples who often use this term, notably the Maori peoples in Aotearoa/New Zealand. The term "Aboriginal" was coined by colonial governments as a catch-all label, and some Indigenous people avoid this term because of its colonial derivation.

communities as not transferable, relevant, or even desirable within the cultural enclaves, socioeconomic conditions, and often remote geographic settings of many First Nations and Inuit communities. First Nations communities have also experienced the difficulties and risks of sending community members away to colleges and universities for long periods of study. Away from the supports of their home communities and unused to urban centres, many of those who leave home do not complete their degree programs. Those who do often do not return to their home communities. For the small percentage who complete their educational program away from home and then return, the relevance of what they have learned may be questioned locally. Such a dynamic can be viewed as educational complicity in community capacity depletion, as opposed to capacity building.

"What of Us Is in Here?"

Virtually none of the available ECCD curricula in Canada includes information specific to the First Nations communities that have asked us to partner with them to construct a culturally specific curriculum. Some Canadian and American institutions providing ECCD training have responded to popular demand for culturally sensitive curricula by introducing purportedly pan-Aboriginal information (Taylor, Crago, and McAlpine 2001). Typically, generalizations are made about the ways of life and beliefs of a conglomerate of Aboriginal peoples who are presumed to be relatively homogeneous – or at least whose distinctive characteristics, circumstances, and goals are taken to be too inconsequential for ECCD program providers to differentiate.

A "beads and feathers" approach (Whyte 1982) to increasing the purported multicultural flavour of curriculum has also been taken, involving adding on bits and pieces of cultural lore about the Cree, Dene, Mohawk, Haida, Ojibway, and a potpourri of other distinct Indigenous populations.

When the Meadow Lake Tribal Council reviewed the available ECCD programs, they were unimpressed with these superficial reflections of difference. They wanted to know, "What of us – our Cree and Dene cultures – is in these programs? How are the particular needs and circumstances of our communities going to be addressed?" These questions provided the stimulus for the First Nations Partnership Programs.

In proposing the initial partnership, the Meadow Lake Tribal Council sought an innovative ECCD training program that would reflect the nine First Nations it represents by incorporating and advancing cherished aspects of their Cree and Dene cultures, languages, traditions, and goals for children: "We must rediscover our traditional values – of caring, sharing, and living in harmony – and bring them into our daily lives and practices" (Ray Ahenakew, executive director, Meadow Lake Tribal Council, personal communication). The importance of involving constituent Meadow Lake communities by allowing them to speak for themselves and bring their particular priorities and practices to the process was a guiding principle: "The prime focus of this project was developing child care services at the community level which would be administered and operated by the communities. As Tribal Council staff, we could not make the error of walking into any of the communities to show them the correct and only way of doing things" (M.R. Opekokew and M. McCallum, personal communication).

Because the Elders are the bearers of traditional knowledge in their communities, it was clear to Meadow Lake Tribal Council from the outset that the curriculum structure would need to provide opportunities to integrate the Elders' teachings into the program. In eight of ten partnership programs to date, Elders have played significant roles in bringing cultural content, historical knowledge, and their experience with generations of the community's children and families into the classroom on a regular basis. The Elders' participation helps ensure that students develop practical perspectives and skills that are informed by the culture and appropriate to the community where they will work after graduation. As one student from the Meadow Lake program said, "Students who took this program have learned a lot about how our cultures think about children, and what they have learned will make a difference to our children and grandchildren. I believe our children – our future – are going to get back on the right track."[3]

Regardless of who asks the question "What of us is in here?" modernist education is focused on what learners are presumed to lack, rather than on what they bring to the endeavour. The intent of modernism, be it in ECCD training and service delivery or in other educational enterprises, is to transmit pre-established ideas – knowledge that is presumed to be immutable and universally significant – as well as to prescribe the parameters that will guide the creation of "new knowledge." By disregarding the voices and experiences of individuals and groups, modernist education is a powerful vehicle for shaping unidimensional understandings of the world. Yet

---

3   Interviews with instructors and students conducted from 1998 to 2000 as part of a comprehensive research study of the first seven partnership programs illuminated some of the conditions that enable successful teaching and learning. Excerpts from these interviews are quoted extensively in this book.

singular notions of truth and the best are inadequate for understanding a world of multiple, reciprocally influencing causes and effects that are rooted in an infinite array of historical and cultural specificities (Lather 1991).

While the innovative work described in this book did not take form in the crucible of postmodernist thought, it can be understood within that discourse (Ball and Pence 2000; Dahlberg, Moss, and Pence 1999). The openness of the Meadow Lake Tribal Council to draw on multiple cultural inputs to co-construct understandings of child development and care gave rise to an exploration of the postmodern as it applies to a tertiary-level ECCD training program.

Guiding Principles

From the outset, the First Nations Partnership Programs team at the University of Victoria's School of Child and Youth Care has seen its role as developing a model for generating curricula in collaboration with communities in a way that, while demonstrated with partnering First Nations communities in Canada, could be used in partnerships with other communities elsewhere and in other human service fields. The First Nations Partnership Program currently consists of twenty university-accredited courses, including five practica, that cover topics equivalent to those offered in mainstream college and university programs for preparing ECCD practitioners, which are delivered by and in communities. There, they are enriched by the cultural teachings and experiential wisdom of Elders and other community-based resource people. Each course includes a structure of activities and assignments, including weekly sessions in which students meet with Elders and other carriers of the First Nations culture and experience to discuss specific areas related to child and youth care and development. Because of the generative curriculum, in no two partnerships has the program delivery or the generated curriculum looked exactly the same. Table 1 shows the career and educational ladder in terms of various credentials that students can obtain through the First Nations Partnership Program. Students can step off the ladder at several junctures along the post-secondary coursework continuum, with a credential at each juncture that makes them eligible for new vocational opportunities. Table 2 shows the sequence of courses that make up the two-year post-secondary program.

While agreeing that consensus on what is of value in curriculum content and activities was not required, we developed with our First Nations partners a set of guiding principles to serve as navigation points in uncharted waters. These principles are:

- support and reinforcement for community initiative in a community-based setting
- bi/multicultural respect
- identification of community and individual strengths as the basis for initiatives
- the ensuring of a broad ecological perspective and an awareness of the child as part of a family and a community
- provision of educational and career laddering for students such that credit for this coursework is fully applicable to future study and practice
- awareness that while the immediate focus is on ECCD, this training should provide the basis for a broader range of training and services for children, youth, families, and communities.

TABLE 1

A child and youth care career and educational ladder

Coursework	Professional status	Responsibilities
40-hour introduction to becoming a family day care provider	Pre-professional	Daily operation of a family daycare program under central First Nations agency supervision.
1-year early childhood education certificate (provided by BC Ministry of Health)	Para-professional Early childhood care and development / Year 1	Supervise child care programs for 3- to 5-year-olds. Staff programs for 0- to 5-year-olds.
2-year university diploma in child and youth care	Professional Early childhood care and development / Year 2	Supervise and staff programs for 0- to 5-year-olds, including children with special needs.
3-year child and youth care courses	Professional Early childhood care and development – Child and youth care / Year 3	Plan, administer, and staff programs for children and youth.
4-year bachelor's degree in child and youth care	Professional Early childhood care and development – Child and youth care / Year 4	Plan, administer, supervise, and staff a wide range of child and youth care programs.

TABLE 2

Generative curriculum in early childhood care and development

Child and youth care strand	Communication skills strand	Child development strand	Practicum strand
Introduction to play	Interpersonal Communications	Child Development I	Practicum 1: Community Care Settings for Children and Youth
Foundations of Curriculum Planning	Communicating with Children and Guiding Children's Behaviour	Child Development II	Practicum 2: The Whole Child
Curriculum Design and Implementation	The Caring and Learning Environment	Introduction to Human Behaviour	Practicum 3: The Child in the Curriculum
The Ecology of Health, Safety and Nutrition	Introduction to Planned Change	Program Development for Infants and Toddlers	Practicum 4: Developmental Specialization Practicum for Working with Infants and Toddlers
Administration of Child Care Facilities	Communication Skills for Professional Helpers	Supported Child Care for Children with Special Needs	Practicum 5: Supported Child Care

These principles articulate the partners' shared belief that a cooperative and co-constructionist approach is not only desirable but necessary. Through these principles we commit ourselves to a position that multiple truths must be respectfully represented in this program and that such knowledge must come through the people who live it. A critical characteristic of the First Nations Partnership Programs is a willingness for the partners to take a risk – and to depend on one another's support in doing so. Partnerships with members of the dominant culture have been problematic for Aboriginal people. Most often they have been required over time, implicitly or explicitly, to accommodate to the dominant culture and to act as if assimilated. This dynamic is one that neither the First Nations with whom we have partnered nor we at the university have wanted to repeat.

Some of our guiding principles, such as educational laddering, reflect structural issues in Canadian post-secondary education that the university partner must take the lead in addressing. Most, though, involve a joint role for both partners. In addition, the partnerships operate within some constraints – for example, the need for the program to be viewed as academically credible and rigorous, and the need to meet provincially legislated licensing and accreditation criteria within the province while ensuring the appropriateness of the knowledge within a community context.

What has emerged from the application of these principles is an approach to generating ECCD practice that project team members have referred to as "community and culturally appropriate practice" – an approach that truly embodies a community's values, choices, and goals for caring for its children. As a Meadow Lake program administrator notes, "Curricula that are not respectful of cultural diversity, that do not acknowledge that there are many trails that lead up the mountain, cannot expect to generate the pride and self-respect necessary to develop caring caregivers."

Grounding ECCD Capacity Building in Culture and Community

Community development has never been the goal of post-secondary practitioner training or of mainstream conceptualizations of ECCD programming. The Generative Curriculum Model, which values being true to the spirit of the partnership and to the community's desires to reclaim and reform, violates assumptions of modernist academia and its historical foundation in doctrines of revealed truth (Pence et al. 1993). As long as truth is conceived as singular and revealed, rather than as multiple and constructed, there is little room for accommodation of the beliefs and values of culturally distinct others. By challenging and confronting established assumptions in a forum that depends on community involvement and dialogue, the Generative Curriculum Model provides elements of an other-than-modernist model of education that imbues learners with a respect for many truths (Ball and Pence 2000). Rather than seeking consensus, the goal of the Generative Curriculum Model is to engender community dialogue, exploration, and testing of the validity and desirability of concepts and practices in the context of the community, in a manner similar to that called for by Indigenous educators Armstrong (2000), Battiste (2000), and Cajete (1999).

A basic assumption of the Generative Curriculum Model, consistent with critiques of developmental psychology by Burman (1994), Cole (1996),

Kagitcibasi (1996) and Nsamenang (1992, 2004), is that no empirical or logical bases exist to assume the validity of theories and research findings about child development across cultures, socio-political conditions, or geographic contexts. Thus, we cannot presume the universal appropriateness of various strategies of promoting children's growth and development that have been effective in largely middle-class European and North American settings, as a growing number of ECCD leaders have argued (Bernhard 1995; Dahlberg, Moss, and Pence 1999; Lubeck and Post 2000a; Moss and Pence 1994; Penn 1997, 2005; Swadener and Kessler 1991; Woodhead 1996). The objectives and methods of child care embody and either reproduce or change the culture in which children and caregivers live and work. Hence, significantly different but equally useful and valued ways may exist to encourage and respond to children across diverse communities and cultural groups (Ball and Pence 1999, 2000; Chang et al. 2000; Derman-Sparks and Phillips 1997; Gonzalez-Mena 2001; Lamb et al. 1992; Pence 1998; Rogoff 2003; Rosenthal 2003; Swadener 2000; Tobin, Wu, and Davidson 1989; Valsiner and Litvinovic 1996; Woodhead, Faulkner, and Littleton 1998).

Illustrating the construct of distributed knowledge elaborated by Lubeck and Post (2000a), students in the training program, their instructors, community supporters, and the university-based team collaborate in the context of each community's visions for their children to share their knowledge, experiences, and skills, working incrementally toward the goal of elaborating curricula and program designs that address the community's particular needs and goals for nurturing children. Thus, the Generative Curriculum Model refocuses attention from the false promise of universality to the reality of diversity. As ECCD specialist Kofi Marfo (1993) remarked when asked to critically review the Meadow Lake program: "I have found the ... project to be one of the most innovative and well conceptualized approaches to addressing the educational and personnel preparation needs of cultural minority communities I have come across ... The curriculum model acknowledges the limits of the knowledge base the principal investigators bring to the project, while appropriately respecting and honoring the tremendous contributions that Elders, students, and community members at large can make to the program."

The Generative Curriculum Model involves communities in mutual learning, sharing of skills, and collaborative construction of concepts and curricula needed to initiate new programs that foster the well-being of children and families within their communities. By supporting the skills and processes required for effective, community-supportive, and community-involving practices, the Generative Curriculum Model has had demonstrated impacts on community commitment, confidence, and the capacity to improve conditions for children and families.

The First Nations communities that have initiated partnerships with us at the University of Victoria have done so with an understanding that the ways to enhance conditions for their children's well-being might not match either Western best practices or the traditions of their Indigenous forebears. The Generative Curriculum Model builds an open curriculum that sits between two cultures, allowing both the message and the medium from each to enter the training process (Ball and Pence 1999; Pence and McCallum 1994). A community-based instructor in the Lil'wat Nation program notes: "We don't have all the answers. In a generative program, we can enjoy learning about what research on child development has shown and what methods seem to be helpful in certain situations. And we can delve further into our own history and traditions, and see how these can help us with our children." A Meadow Lake Tribal Council Elder describes the bicultural features of the Generative Curriculum Model as "two sides of an eagle feather," pointing out that "both are needed to fly."

Co-Constructing Quality through Dialogue and Praxis

Most post-secondary education requires two bodies of participants: students and representatives (instructors, administrators) of the post-secondary institution. The approach innovated in the First Nations Partnership Programs requires the addition of a third participating body – the student's community. A key characteristic of the partnership process is that the curriculum generated through it is open to and respectful of information from academia, from the community, and, potentially, from other sources as well. Elaboration of the curriculum for each course in the training program involves members of the community and the university working together to incorporate knowledge from the mainstream of theory, research, and practice pertaining to early childhood and from the communities represented by the First Nations band or tribal council. A student in the Lil'wat Nation program describes the approach succinctly: "Being in this program is like having the best of both worlds. We love to learn about what researchers have found out about child development and such from our textbooks, and we love to learn more about our own culture and how we can use it to help the children of our community."

In contrast to the assumptions of community deficiencies that underlie many expert-driven approaches to professional training and service delivery, an empowerment approach assumes that "all families have strengths and that much of the most valid and useful knowledge about the rearing of children can be found in the community itself – across generations, in networks, and in ethnic and cultural traditions" (Cochran 1988, 144). The principles of respect and voice that guide the work of partnership within a caring, supportive, and inclusive educational environment approximate Benhabib's (1992) principle of egalitarian reciprocity.

Although students in a partnership program using the Generative Curriculum Model learn about mainstream theories, research, and practice pertaining to ECCD, the partnership approach to generating ECCD training curriculum does not rest on modernist assumptions about universally shared goals for children or caregivers or about common pathways toward optimal developmental outcomes. Rather, in the manner called for by a growing number of postmodernist and other than modernist educators and developmental psychologists (e.g., Bloch and Popkewitz 2000; Dasen and Jahoda 1986; Green 1993; Kagitcibasi 1996; Kessler and Hauser 2000; Lubeck 1996, 1998; Lubeck and Post 2000b; Nsamenang 1992, 2004; Steffe and Gayle 1995; Swadener and Kessler 1991), students explore diverse possibilities of the meaning and implications of development for caregivers within the context of their own culture and community. They are routinely asked to engage with questions of goodness of fit of various concepts and practices in ECCD. Through continuous input from and dialogue with Elders and other community members, and through the physical proximity of the children and families through which the community's culture is embodied, students are constantly challenged to work the tensions between high theory and everyday practice (Lather 1991).

Valuing process over product and construction over prescription, students, instructors, and community resource people in the program engage with questions rather than prescriptive answers about the correct ways to encourage children's development and handle challenging situations. As described in detail later in this book, the pedagogical approach is constructivist (Steffe and Gayle 1995). Teaching is guided by the principles of active and interactive learning and discovery, necessitating and celebrating dialogue among the various perspectives in a manner also described by Bernhard (1995), Bernhard et al. (1998), Brookfield and Preskill (1999), Goffin (1996), Gonzalez-Mena (2001), Jones (1994), Kessler and Swadener (1992), Pacini-Ketchabaw and McIvor (2005), and others. Students are actively involved in an ongoing process of articulating, comparing, and sometimes combining perspectives contributed by members of their own community and by the university-based curriculum team.

As a partner, the University of Victoria brings to the training program a representative sample of theory, research, and practical approaches to ECCD from the largely middle-class, Euro-North American mainstream. These materials have value, as a community-based instructor of a partnership program with Treaty 8 Tribal Association in northern British Columbia notes: "The course material really supports the instructor by giving ideas to follow and suggestions of activities and resources. But it's also flexible enough to allow us to adapt it to the needs of this particular group of students and the communities and cultures they are part of."

As a partner, the First Nations community brings knowledge of its culture, values, practices, and (sometimes) language, as well as its vision of optimal child development and its perspective on how best to facilitate healthy development. In the words of a community-based program administrator: "We can consider what mainstream theories say and if we [choose] to believe them and use them in our work, that doesn't make us less Indian. And if we [choose] to assert the importance of our cultural traditions and ways of raising children, that doesn't make us wrong. This program recognizes and encourages this give and take, pick and choose. It doesn't cage us and expect us to act like Europeans."

First Nations and university partners agree that the curriculum should not emerge based solely on a consideration of community-based perspectives and practices. Even within cultures, individuals carry different messages, knowledge, and forms for conveying that information. Furthermore, not all of the relevant information exists "in community." The generative curriculum needs to be suspended in the space between, in the void – the unfilled space that is charged with potential (Pence 1999a). This space is one that is respectful of many voices and perspectives. As one instructor explains, the generative program offers a learning experience for all individuals participating, including the community-based instructors, who can explore their knowledge through generating a curriculum, and who are given new tools and methods with which to share their history and traditions with the next generations.

By bringing together the worlds of Western academia and Indigenous communities, plausible alternatives to Euro-North American modernist ways of conceptualizing child development and care are created. Some of these alternatives build on each other, stimulating additional changes and new directions throughout the generative curriculum process. Thus, there is a synchronous, mutually stimulating co-occurrence of learning, developing, and teaching the curriculum and of formulating culturally resonant programs for children and families in the students' own community. Greater understanding of the potential fit and utility of alternative constructions comes, in part, from an appreciation of the varying contexts from which different concepts, findings, and child care models emerge, as well as from greater sensitivity to the history, socio-political positioning, conditions, and evolving goals of the communities in which trained ECCD practitioners are likely to work. The recursive consideration of these different views – the seeking out of what Freire (1970/1993) would call "new knowledge" – represents the heart of the Generative Curriculum Model. The goal is not to progress toward a state of consensus or completion, with the risk of formalizing an ossified curriculum similar to those on offer in most educational institutions. Instead, the ongoing dialogical, process-driven approach of participatory praxis which is the essence of the Generative Curriculum Model has the potential to create a new "generation" at each delivery – a living, responsive, evolving curriculum.

Our experiences with First Nations communities in Canada suggest that when we truly grasp the significance of taking community and culture into consideration and put this principle into practice, we can no longer engage in the business-as-usual delivery of mainstream ECCD programs, no matter how adequately they respond to research and theory reported in mainstream literature and lecture halls about the developmental needs of children studied by Euro-Western psychologists and educators. Being responsive to communities and sensitive to culture means opening the foundations of how training programs are conceived, of how optimal developmental outcomes are defined. It means transforming our training from a prepackaged, didactic process to one that is open-ended and participatory. It means engaging in dialogue, co-constructing curricula that will further a community's own internally identified goals, sharing the floor in course delivery, and moving over so that communities can determine the desired end products of training. In the words of Vern Bachiu of Meadow Lake Tribal Council: "What we are trying to do is turn the world upside down."

Harnessing the Potential
of Partnership

Partnering ... requires the perception that each partner has something
of value both to give and to receive.

– M. Kerr (1998)

Partnership in the Learning Community

"Partnership" has become a buzzword in the human services, yet genuine
partnership is rare. It requires us to abandon conventional donor-recipient
models and adopt an intention to work with our partners toward a goal of
mutual improvement (Kerr 1998, 4). The commitment to work in partnership is a conscious decision to harness the potential that exists in the networks of relationships that define us as human beings. This commitment
requires us to open ourselves to the possibility of mutual transformation
and to focus our attention on the resources that are available from moment to moment – in ourselves, in our partners, and in the environment –
to support a dynamic, unfolding partnership process.

The strength of the Generative Curriculum Model lies in its capacity to
support the development of meaningful partnerships. Partnerships constitute the model's underlying unity; they are inextricably linked to the processes of generating knowledge, learning and teaching, revitalizing cultural
pride, strengthening communities, and transforming individuals and institutions. Thus, the Generative Curriculum Model is not a program in the
conventional sense, although it includes elements that might be thought
of as such – for example, a set of courses that add up to a diploma. The
Generative Curriculum Model's guiding principles, taken together, have
the potential to set in motion a process from which unique programs can

emerge according to the needs, aspirations, and strengths of diverse communities. That process is driven forward at every stage by the evolution of dynamic partnerships within and between communities. As these partnerships develop, the structural elements of the First Nations Partnership Program – for example, the open-ended curriculum that supports the twenty courses – give purpose and opportunity to that independently evolving process, which differs in each community. In other words, both the program and the character of the partnership emerge through the process of delivery, supported by partners who come to feel that their own and their communities' lives are connected to, and reflected in, that process. The courses and the curriculum aid in this delivery but are not themselves "the program"; rather, the program is *generated* through the process. Each resulting program is unique, but the underlying principles and common structural elements that assist each successive delivery lend a kind of family resemblance.

First Nations Partnership Programs: An Overview
Since 1989, the University of Victoria has entered into ten partnerships with nine Aboriginal organizations representing more than sixty First Nations communities. These partnerships, which share certain processes and structures, have come to be known collectively as the First Nations Partnership Programs (see Table 3).

Each partnership is initiated by a First Nations community. Most often, communities want to train child and youth care staff for a new child care centre or for related child and family services, and they seek the expertise of the First Nations Partnership Programs team at the University of Victoria. Together, the university team and the partnering community develop a program, based on a set of specified courses, to suit that community's child and youth care needs. Sometimes, at the tribal partner's request, a regional educational institution gets involved as well. This was the case in the partnerships with the Cowichan Tribes, Nzen'man' Child and Family Services, and Onion Lake First Nation.

Diane Bigfoot, education director for Treaty 8 Tribal Association, describes a fairly typical entry to the First Nations Partnership Programs:

> After an initial visit by education society members to see the Cowichan program, we went to [the University of Victoria] to meet with Alan Pence and Jessica Ball. We liked the approach of the generative curriculum, which we found more relevant to our community. We really got excited about it. We saw the write-ups from the Meadow Lake experience, and we talked about it.

We were quite impressed with our meeting there, and came back and decided that was the route to go. It was going to give us more relevant training, and that would be better for our communities and our students. We did not want to send our students out of the region.

The First Nations communities conduct their own application and preparatory programs for students based on locally established criteria and assessment procedures. Common student selection criteria include fluency in written and spoken English, a level of academic preparedness that suggests a high probability of program completion, personal health and stability, positive relationships with children through work or family, and a strong career interest in ECCD.

TABLE 3

First Nations Partnership Programs, diploma deliveries, 1989-2006

First Nations partner	Local partnering institution	Location	Program duration
Meadow Lake Tribal Council		Meadow Lake, SK	1989-93
Cowichan Tribes	Malaspina University-College	Duncan, BC	1993-95
Nzen'man' Child and Family Services	Nicola Valley Institute of Technology	Lytton, BC	1995-97
Onion Lake First Nation	Saskatchewan Indian Institute of Technologies	Onion Lake, SK	1996-98
Tl'azt'en Nation		Tache, BC	1996-99
Treaty 8 Tribal Association		Fort St. John, BC	1997-99
Lil'wat Nation		Mount Currie, BC	1997-99
Little Shuswap Indian Band		Chase, BC	2000-02
Little Shuswap Indian Band		Chase, BC	2002-04
Penelakut Tribe		Kuper Island, BC	2003-06

Candidates for the program are typically women with a keen interest in children's well-being. Most, but not all, have completed high school. The First Nations communities recruit the candidates, who are identified and then recommended to the university-based program coordinator as a cohort (that is, as a group from the partnering communities who will journey through the whole program together). A "mature student" admissions procedure is arranged by the University of Victoria in which flexible prior learning criteria are used. The university team reviews the applications and enrols eligible students in a two-year Aboriginal diploma program in child and youth care at the University of Victoria. The cohort size of the first ten partnerships has ranged from ten to twenty-two students.

In three-way partnerships involving a local college, instructors are typically co-selected by the community and the two institutions. In two of the partnership programs, the University of Victoria initially handled course accreditation and student registration; in a third case, the local college (Saskatchewan Indian Institute of Technologies) registered the students.

Whenever possible, course instructors are local to the community. Qualified instructors are recruited and contracted by the First Nations partner and approved by the academic institution. At least one instructor in each of the partnership programs to date has been a certified specialist in early childhood education (ECE). The university team helps orient the instructors and provides detailed course material for the university-level courses. Specific activities designed to draw out community participation and knowledge are written into this curriculum.

The First Nations community coordinates the all-important participation of local Elders and respected others. Most community partners recruit an intergenerational facilitator who understands community protocol for asking Elders to participate in the program. Elders join in the teaching process either in the classroom or by allowing students to visit them in their homes to discuss topics that are part of each course. Each community has a slightly different way of identifying who is an Elder. Generally, Elders are older adults who have demonstrated to community members that they possess knowledge and a wise perspective on the community's history and cultural identity.

A core group of about five community members usually emerges early in the partnership to move into place the elements needed to enable program delivery. This steering committee typically responds to input and feedback from a larger group within the community, such as an education or daycare society, employment and training board, or band chief and councillors. In each community, one or two persons act as the primary liaisons with the University of Victoria's First Nations Partnership Programs team.

The community identifies suitable, accessible practicum sites where students can develop applied competencies. Practicum supervisors at these sites are recruited by First Nations community administrators. The supervisors are important, not only because successful practica are required by the provincial government to qualify for ECE certification, but also because students depend on them to provide a safe and non-discriminatory atmosphere where they can develop new skills.

Throughout the life of a program, the First Nations Partnership Programs team works with community counterparts to ensure the program's success by responding to the needs of the students, instructors, administrators, and Elders, as well as of the community at large. The team includes the authors (Alan and Jessica) and, typically, three part-time staff. Staff are involved in curriculum writing, revision, and updating. One team member looks after administrative requirements such as student registrations, submission of grades, and any communications required to maintain operations. Community liaison is another important role. The roles and responsibilities of the partners with respect to program planning, delivery, and evaluation are summarized in Table 4.

Each partnership includes a pre-program phase of interaction with the communities. During this phase, which ranges from one to five years, a supportive ecology develops. Several factors affect the length of the pre-program phase: the level of prior knowledge among community leaders about possible training models, which affects the time required for program selection and mobilization; community organization and the availability of leaders to become involved; accessibility of funding needed by the community to mount the program; the number of competing interests or initiatives in the community; and the frequency and severity of disruptive events in the community affecting the pace and focus of pre-program preparation.

The preparatory activities undertaken in the pre-program phase – and the many challenges they present – are vital to program success. Personal relationships of trust, reciprocity, and mutual assistance develop during this time that affect whether a program will come to fruition. Accessing funding is an important activity, and it is often a demanding task for First Nations communities because sources of funds are limited, competition for funds can be intense, and the amount of time required to complete an

TABLE 4

Roles and responsibilities of community and university partners

First Nations communities	University of Victoria
Initiate partnership based on needs and objectives of community members	Ensure academic accreditation (course ladder and education career ladder)
Secure program funding	Liaise with program administrators (point of entry for third partner)
Administer preparatory programs and full training program	Appoint instructors
Recruit student cohort and instructors	Register student cohort
Employ instructors and inter-generational facilitator	Provide curriculum resources using the Generative Curriculum Model
Co-construct bicultural ECCD curriculum	Co-construct bicultural ECCD curriculum
Deliver program (classrooms/practica)	Design and conduct program evaluation
Provide ongoing support for students	Prepare and disseminate information on partnership programs
Participate in documentation and evaluation	

application, receive a response, and, when necessary, resubmit can be exhausting and disheartening. Administrators in one partnership program approached almost twenty potential sponsors before funding was secured.

Informing community members about the proposed program and mobilizing broadly based community interest and support are also critical, as is establishing a shared vision of the partnership's mission and the specific goals to be achieved. To support each project, partners must clarify and confirm agreements about core features of the program model and the content. We achieve this clarity through an interactive process that is stimulated by discussion of a proposed Memorandum of Understanding. This memorandum includes the guiding principles of the Generative Curriculum Model, the courses that will be offered in the First Nations Partnership Program, and the credentials that will be attainable. Clarifying partner roles and responsibilities and obtaining approvals from administrative representatives of the partnering post-secondary institutions are also critical pre-program components.

In addition to co-constructing a supportive ecology and a broad frame-work for program delivery, all of the concrete elements that will enable program implementation are moved into place during the pre-program phase. These elements include selection of a student cohort; recruitment of intergenerational facilitators, instructors, Elders, and practicum super-visors; and establishment of the program funding and budget.

Every partnering community provides some preparatory programs for students during the pre-program phase. These preparatory programs, which include upgrading academic skills and introductions to ECE, range from two weeks to one year in length. Students in the preparatory programs have experienced variable success in previous schooling. Those who have attempted post-secondary programs have often had disappointing experi-ences that eroded their self-confidence. First Nations cultures are often described as oral cultures, and students often need to become more adept at reading and writing to succeed in post-secondary education. Prepara-tory programs developed according to the principles of the Generative Curriculum Model and delivered by the institutional partners are a key part of building relationships and establishing the community-involving approach to the education program.

Instructors in the First Nations Partnership Programs find the exten-sive curriculum materials provided by the university team during the pre-program phase to be an indispensable asset in preparing and supporting them with a range of options for covering course material and for involving Elders. Instructors who have moved into a community to teach in the pro-gram have emphasized that the social challenges faced early in the program could be eased by pre-program orientation and assistance with integration into the community. Challenges instructors face include cross-cultural com-munication and adaptation to cultural forms of interaction, safety concerns, and becoming sufficiently accepted by the community to be able to work with Elders and other community resource people in the co-constructive curriculum process. One instructor notes:

> I just lucked out that my temperament allowed me to fit in. We've all talked about how nervous we were at first, because we just have a different style. So if I had been prepared for that at the beginning, it would have been better. I just waited, and listened and sat back, and I think we came to a pretty good understanding of how to communicate with each other ... But it took time ... we're only looking out our own window ... Unless you know what the other person is seeing out their window, you're always questioning it ... Whereas if you can really communicate what you're seeing out your window then you're

right on track. And people don't get right down to that. You wait for a long time to interpret what people are seeing. (Instructor, Tl'azt'en Nation)

Most community-based administrators in the programs have not previously been involved in delivering an on-site post-secondary program. A tremendous amount of work is involved leading up to formalization of the partnership and program start-up. Establishing community agency in implementing program delivery in the community setting and involving as many community members as possible is essential during this early stage of engagement. Subsequent to the First Nations Partnership Programs, a number of the communities have pursued other training programs, where they have continued to have a strong say in the nature of the delivery.

The success of the pre-program phase is critical to the overall effectiveness of each partnership: the conditions that will enable effective program delivery are established during this important period before the program is actually implemented. A large number of unknowns characterize this initial phase, which can make it stressful and challenging, and so it is essential that a comprehensive and systematic approach be taken to prepare communities and instructors for the highly participatory program that values community members' contributions of cultural knowledge.

Throughout the course of ten partnership programs, and particularly during the pre-program phase, we have found a number of attitudes and forms of interpersonal engagement essential to the effectiveness of our role as the institutional partner. In particular, we have found it important to:

- tolerate high levels of uncertainty and shared control of the program
- clarify and confirm informally, and later formally, agreement about the partnership's mission and core program elements
- make a long-term commitment and persevere
- respond to expressions of community needs regarding program implementation with a high level of flexibility
- be self-critical and willing to jettison the "excess baggage" of our institution to work around some of its constraints
- become familiar with the communities' priorities, practices, and circumstances without becoming involved in them (i.e., we did not seek or presume to become experts or insiders of the cultures or social life of the community partners)
- assume an encouraging, non-directive stance while waiting

- avoid "doing" when non-action would be more productive of community agency and, ultimately, capacity building
- be receptive to what communities bring to individual projects, although these contributions may come in unfamiliar forms and at unexpected times (Ball 2000).

Each partnership program takes unexpected twists and turns. Given our previous experience not only with the Generative Curriculum Model but also with other post-secondary education in child and youth care, we have been tempted at times to intervene when we felt a program was getting off track. However, intervention would almost certainly have undermined communities' efforts to work together to create local solutions to local needs. Their trust in us as partners who respect their autonomy would also have been damaged. Moreover, valuable opportunities would have been missed to empower communities to marshal their own strengths in pursuit of a common goal. We have learned much about the limitations of our own professional biases in this process. As a Meadow Lake Tribal Council administrator puts it, "You can't just get out ahead of the communities. A program needs to be not only community-based but community-paced."

The Emergence of the Unique

By stepping back as communities implement the Generative Curriculum Model in their own time, in their own way, we have had the opportunity to witness ten distinct partnership programs evolve, each with its own character shaped, in part, by the communities' responses to events that transpired over the course of their programs. While the programs share common elements, each has its particular strengths. For example, while every program involves Elders to some degree, Elders' participation was strongest in the partnerships with Meadow Lake Tribal Council, the Cowichan Tribes, and Lil'wat Nation. Some of the programs have enjoyed high community visibility (the partnership with the Cowichan Tribes being particularly strong in this regard) while others with a lower community profile (such as the program with Nzen'man' Child and Family Services) developed a particularly strong and mutually supportive student cohort. During the partnership with Tl'azt'en Nation, half of the twelve students gave birth and virtually every student in the program experienced the violent death of a relative. Despite these personal challenges, the students showed extraordinary resilience. While most of the partnership programs are delivered in the students' home communities, the partnership with Treaty 8

Tribal Association illustrates that the model can still work in cases where students might need to move to a central location to overcome the challenges posed by distance between participating communities. These are but a few ways in which the partnership programs have evolved in distinct but successful ways according to the strengths and resources of individual communities.

Programs have also differed in the number of major partners involved. For example, the initial partnership with Meadow Lake and six additional programs have been two-way partnerships between a First Nations organization and the University of Victoria. This structure has several advantages: fewer people need to develop working relationships; communications are streamlined; and there is an increase in the transparency of the institutional partner, which eases the complexity of liaison by community administrators.

This two-way structure has not been adopted by all First Nations partners. Three programs thus far have been three-way partnerships involving the First Nations organization that implemented and directed the program, the University of Victoria, which provided the Generative Curriculum Model and the curriculum resources, and a community college that directly supported program implementation in the community. Three-way partnerships are more complex and require more communication to clarify purposes and procedures. However, they enable communities to forge a broader network of mutually supportive parties for the capacity-building endeavour and extend the reach of new learning about how to partner effectively. This is especially important for post-secondary institutions, where many program arrangements guided by the Generative Curriculum Model, such as a cohort-driven approach and co-constructing curriculum with Elders, break new ground. Two of our college partners, Saskatchewan Indian Institute of Technologies and Malaspina University-College, have continued to deliver Generative Curriculum Model coursework after their initial delivery of the First Nations Partnership Program. The three-way partnerships with the Cowichan Tribes and Nzen'man' Child and Family Services illustrate some of the challenges and opportunities presented by three-way partnerships.

Nzen'man' Child and Family Services Partnership

The Nzen'man' Child and Family Services agency addresses the needs of about thirty-five hundred First Nations people in eleven bands spread over a three-hundred-square-kilometre area on the east and west sides of British Columbia's Fraser River canyon. The agency wanted a locally based training program that would enable First Nations people to operate a child care centre and create other service programs for First Nations families. They entered into a three-way partnership with the University of Victoria and the Nicola Valley Institute of Technology to provide a child and youth care program, in part to explore the feasibility of instituting an ECCD program at this new Indigenous college.

Midway through the partnership, an upheaval within the college administration resulted in students requesting program completion through a two-way partnership with the University of Victoria. Despite these challenges, the program proved fruitful for all participants. For the students, the experience of taking control of the program's direction in the face of difficulties was an exercise in empowerment likely made possible both by the Generative Curriculum Model's promotion of community agency and by bonds of trust between the communities and the University of Victoria. Alfreda Nelson, a graduate of the program, notes:

> I really enjoyed my training program ... and I must say my views have changed. I am not as judgmental; I give both sides their chance to say their view. And I'd say that most of the students have changed for the better. They are more open. I think a lot of us have learned not just to accept what we're told, but to question it sometimes.

We supported the students' choice to relocate the child and youth care training program to the local primary school at Lytton, British Columbia – a move that had unexpected benefits, as many of the students' own children were in classes just down the hall. The day-to-day contact with the children and teachers in the school was a great education in itself: theory, practice, and family life merged. The students became more involved in school affairs as parents, community members, and, eventually, as colleagues. After completing the program, most of the graduates found work in community child care centres and family support programs. Many became involved in their children's school, including one graduate who obtained employment as a preschool teacher. Enhanced self-esteem was a lasting outcome for all of the students in the program.

The experience with the First Nations Partnership Program also proved instructive for the Nicola Valley Institute of Technology. College administrators found their involvement in the partnership to be a useful experience in the institution's evolution. In particular, they recognized the need for accreditation of training modules, the importance of procedures that ensure quality in program delivery, and the value of involving Elders as a strategy for ensuring cultural relevance in curriculum development.

Cowichan Tribes Partnership

The three-way partnership involving the Cowichan Tribes took a very different course from that with Nzen'man' Child and Family Services. The Cowichan Tribes, based in the mid-Vancouver Island town of Duncan, British Columbia, came to the partnership with a substantial record of mounting successful social and economic programs for the Coast Salish people. Consequently, when they initiated a child and youth care training program in 1993, they did so from a position of strength. Among the first ten partnerships, the Cowichan partners exhibited the greatest degree of organization and community involvement in generating community-appropriate, culturally grounded curriculum. They established advisory and curriculum review committees that provided detailed advice on how to integrate First Nations cultural content into the daily lesson plans. A clear understanding existed within the community that, "to ensure that our culture would be reflected in the structure of children's services, we had to bring the training program to the community and bring the community into the training program" (Louise Underwood, intergenerational facilitator, Cowichan Tribes). Right from the start, the Cowichan Council provided a strong contingent of Elders to assist with the program. Ross Modeste, an Elder who participated, commented that "the program [was] a real leap ahead in terms of our culture, especially because we are an oral culture and language is the basis of our culture. This program is helping our people to regain our identity."

The Cowichan Tribes requested a three-way partnership consisting of the University of Victoria, themselves, and Malaspina University-College, which has a campus in Duncan that is located on Cowichan territory. In this program, the local college delivered the curriculum under the guidance of the university; both institutions worked in partnership with the Cowichan tribal structure. Malaspina University-College provided the child and youth care instructors at the Duncan campus and issued the two-year diploma in child and youth care.

This three-way partnership program was successful not only in relation to the child care training program it was designed to support but also with respect to the college's operation as a whole, illustrating the potential for broader partnerships to enrich the wider community over time. In the 1990s, the number of First Nations people attending Malaspina University-College increased significantly, due in part to the pioneering efforts of the partnership program. After the conclusion of the child care training program, and based on the First Nations Partnership Programs' model,

Malaspina University-College established an Elder-in-residence position to better support and serve the First Nations community at its doorstep. Louise Underwood, who had been the intergenerational facilitator for the Cowichan partnership program, was the first Elder to hold this position. Program graduate Yvonne Connelly was employed by the college as a student advisor to help First Nations students achieve their academic and vocational goals in largely non-Indigenous classrooms. Commenting on the significance of the child care training program in her own life, Connelly said:

> The program really encouraged me to participate and interact. I was constantly active with my education and responding to myself as well as my school work. We did interviews in the community, which helped expand my social and family support. Growing up off-reserve and non-status, I always viewed myself as non-Native. Today I view myself as non-status Native. It sounds minor but it's major, and it reclaims who I really am. I found that identity through this course. I have more awareness of self, self-worth, and self-esteem. I have been much more sensitive to others. I have healthier relationships with my family ... You carry your child and youth care training through in your own life and then take it into the outer world ... It really set the foundation.

The Cowichan Tribes project faced many challenges on its way to completion, but evaluations conducted at two points during the program echoed the findings from the Meadow Lake project (see Cook 1993). Widespread community benefits were noted by the Cowichan project evaluator, Adrienne Kemble (in Riggan and Kemble 1994). Midway through the project a student remarked, "This program has a different feeling and atmosphere from mainstream programs." At the conclusion of the two-year program, another student noted, "I really wish the third and fourth years [of the career ladder] were Coast Salish-based. This was a great experience for me." A third student commented, "As a Native program it has greatly impacted on my need to pursue my Native heritage in a more aggressive manner ... It has made a difference in my work with Native youth."

Reflections on Partnership

The First Nations Partnership Programs demonstrate the benefits that can flow when partners recognize the need to anchor capacity-building initiatives deeply within the context of the local people, their existing social organization and cultural strengths, their potential for transformation, and their will to move forward on internally articulated agendas. Many human service initiatives at both the individual and community levels assume that the more chronically oppressed or needy a group of people appears to be, the more that "helping" professionals must bring to the situation. The record of First Nations Partnership Programs illustrates the opposite. Indeed, many of the lessons learned during the course of ten partnership programs run directly counter to conventional practices in post-secondary education and the human services.

Significantly, many of the benefits that have resulted from the First Nations Partnership Programs could not have occurred through the kinds of relationships typically encountered in academic institutions and the "helping" professions – even those that purport to operate within an ethic of partnership and community involvement. In the words of Jenny Whitstone, post-secondary coordinator of the Onion Lake First Nation program:

> I believe that if I had taken these seventeen students and offered the program off-reserve, we would have had a success rate of 20 or 25 percent [instead of the 100 percent success rate that was achieved]. So what is the difference? Is it because we offered it here? That's one reason. I think it is also due to the generative curriculum. What that implies to me is more than just a book curriculum. Much more than academia. I think it is a total involvement of the community in ways such as bringing in Elders, making the community part of this. The way that it was offered was unique.

Practices typically associated with social services training and professionalization generally militate against working with and through communities. Many people agree in theory with the goals of partnership but fail to recognize that genuine partnership cannot be achieved through conventional avenues. Real partnership requires an active and respectful engagement in cooperative planning with the communities of which we are a part – learning to do *with* and not *to* those with whom we live and work. Professionals and experts must be prepared to be knowledgeable, supportive, involved co-participants engaged with communities as listeners as well as speakers, as followers as well as leaders. As co-participants, professionals must become comfortable with the indeterminacy and power sharing that co-construction requires.

To be supportive of community efforts to strengthen capacity, institutional partners and community leaders themselves must be scrupulous not to pre-empt or to overwhelm the community with goods and services imported from outside the community context and out of step with its internal rhythms and pace. The potential exists in any community for passive receptivity and eventual dependency; capacity-building initiatives must therefore capitalize on community agency.

Institutions, investigators, and program planners can contribute to cultural sustainability by collaborating with community leaders and groups to build social capital from within the ranks of the youngest to the oldest generations. "All ways" respectful social networks based on trust, reciprocity, and the will to act on behalf of community well-being are fundamental to healthy, sustainable social ecologies in which children and families can thrive. In all ten communities where the Generative Curriculum Model has been piloted, these concepts have been creatively and practically problematized, ultimately enriching all partners in the process. As Brian Opikokew, administrator of Meadow Lake Tribal Council, said, "Everybody walks a lot taller because of this program."

Co-Constructing Curriculum
from the Inside Out

We join spokes together in a wheel,
but it is the center hole that makes the wagon move.
We shape clay into a pot, but it is the emptiness inside that
  holds whatever we want.
We hammer wood for a house,
but it is the inner space that makes it liveable.
We work with being, but non-being is what we use.
                                  – Lao-tzu, *Tao Te Ching*

The Collapse of Objective Knowledge

The training for and provision of social services – particularly in North America – follows an academic and professional heritage based on principles of immutable truth and restricted access to that truth. The traditions of the Enlightenment and of logical positivism are but more recent manifestations of a singular understanding of knowledge, deeply rooted in Western society and its institutions, as a scarce and specific commodity, one that only a few possess in sufficient quality and quantity (1999b).

During the twentieth century, a variety of thinkers (e.g., Foucault 1970; Giroux 1989; Habermas 1983; Kuhn 1970; Lyotard 1984; Toulmin 1990) profoundly critiqued this philosophical tradition, including its fundamental concepts of truth and knowledge. In the past thirty years, this critique has become mainstream within the disciplines of philosophy, literary criticism, the physical sciences and, more recently, the social sciences. Much of the debate has been confined to theory, however. At the level of practice, mainstream notions of truth – as reflected in reliance on "expert knowledge," "professional standards," "objective evaluation," "scientific criteria," and the like – remain essentially unchallenged. Indeed, in many spheres, particularly the social services, their authority appears to be increasing.

Within the field of early childhood care and development (ECCD), many researchers and practitioners have worked to develop best practices that support an often unquestioned modernist conception of child development heavily grounded in North American research, theory, and cultural values. While this work is well intentioned and has value, particularly within a mainstream North American context, it has the potential to stifle other understandings of child, family, and community development, both in mainstream communities and in diverse cultural and ethnic communities in North America and around the globe. Too often, international conferences on early childhood are dominated by theories and research approaches with origins and references in the West, to the neglect of Majority World and Indigenous perspectives. Fortunately, a counter-discourse emerged in the early 1990s that has challenged orthodoxy and enlivened discussions of research and practice (Burman 1994; Kessler and Swadener 1992; Moss and Pence 1994; Penn and Molteno 1997; Woodhead 1996).

While the tenets of professionalism still promote the need for "professional autonomy, self regulation, a specific formal education, and a clientele which recognizes the authority of the profession" (Kelly 1990, 168), the social science bedrock on which such restrictive and exclusionary principles were based has crumbled. As noted by Schwandt, "The epistemology of logical positivism has proved to be untenable. The firm conviction that the world was simply 'out there' waiting to be discovered and described has been exposed as a convenient fiction" (1996, 58). The aftershocks of this Cartesian collapse continue to reverberate throughout the worlds of science and social science. In the social services, these events are often misinterpreted as a revolution – a familiar cycle in history in which an old power system is overthrown, opening the way for its replacement by some faction of the formerly dispossessed. Untransformed in this social services revolution, however, is the core belief that right answers exist, the property now of the formerly disenfranchised who have seized power as the wheel of history turns.

The Generative Curriculum Model is not about revolution; nor is the model a spectre of radical relativism wherein anything goes and experts can be dismissed. The terms "expert" and "professional" must be problematized, however, and their modernist roots exposed and reconstructed in collaboration with those impacted by experts' practice – children, families, and communities. We strongly believe that "quality" must be defined through an inclusionary, not an exclusionary, process. For us, the condition of "Cartesian anxiety" (Bernstein 1983) potentially created by the collapse of so-called objective knowledge can be resolved through what Schwandt (1996) calls "practical philosophy":

> First, inquirers seek to establish a dialogical relationship of openness with participants in the inquiry ... Second, inquirers view the participants in the inquiry as themselves engaged in performing a practical art ... Third, the aim of such inquiry is not to replace practitioners' commonsense knowledge of their respective and joint practices with allegedly more sophisticated, theoretical, scientific knowledge but to encourage practitioners to critically reflect on and reappraise their commonsense knowledge ... Finally, we retain the Enlightenment insight regarding the importance of self-clarity ... but we seek to adopt a better or more critically defensible notion of what this entails. (63-64)

Generating a Living Curriculum

The Generative Curriculum Model embodies the practical philosophy described above. The model places mainstream Western ECCD teachings in dialogue with Indigenous understandings of child care through the participation of Elders and other community members in curriculum generation. We view community involvement in curriculum development in two distinct ways, both of which are important in developing a renewed understanding of knowledge.

In the first view, the generative process in which Elders and other community members contribute First Nations perspectives on child care serves primarily as a means to recognize and include Indigenous knowledge. This is a necessary means because such knowledge is generally not available in written form. It is also an urgent means, given that Indigenous knowledge is at risk of extinction as Elders age and die. This view of the generative process acknowledges the value of diverse cultural understandings of child development and care, as well as the importance of community involvement in knowledge generation, both of which are critical to the integrity of the Generative Curriculum Model. However, it fails to challenge the Western view of knowledge as commodity, as something out there to be discovered.

A second way of viewing the Generative Curriculum Model is to see the generative process itself as intrinsic to a renewed understanding of knowledge – it is more than a means; it is an end in itself. This view questions the concept of knowledge as commodity, suggesting a radically different perception of knowledge as process – a process that necessarily is incomplete, indeterminate, and contingent on both the place and time of the knowing and on the quality of people's participation in it. In the early stages of developing the Generative Curriculum Model, our understanding was informed primarily by the first view. Over the course of the First Nations Partnership Programs, however, we came to see the second view as holding more promise.

In the initial partnership with Meadow Lake Tribal Council, the decision to involve the community in curriculum generation was seen not as radical but as necessary and sensible. No texts or materials existed that could provide information on traditional practices and values within the communities. Indeed, many community members were themselves long estranged from this knowledge. The Tribal Council identified a number of Elders and other respected community members as those who could speak to students about the communities' traditional knowledge. The major focus of this early work, consistent with the Generative Curriculum Model's guiding principles, was to follow and support the community's lead, honouring not only what we at the University of Victoria would bring to the process, but also what the community would provide. This work was critical in shaping a multivocal, inclusive approach to curriculum generation.

The earliest course materials produced were heavily scripted. In each community, student learning and teacher delivery packages typically numbered 100 to 150 pages per course. Each course included thirteen weeks of three hours of instruction per week, plus homework and outside class projects. In this respect, the courses were consistent with modernist education packages like those found in many print-based distance education courses. However, the generative curriculum materials deviated considerably from "normal" practice in the nature of the assignments and in the augmentation of instructor and text information with Elder, student, and community information. This opening up of curriculum came to be described as an "open architecture" approach to curriculum design (Pence 1999a), and it played a significant role in our developing understanding of knowledge as process.

In the Meadow Lake project, one afternoon each week was set aside for the Elders to speak. At first, the course writers suggested topics to complement the course materials for that week. For example, during the week the course addressed perinatal care, an Elder midwife might speak about her experiences and knowledge. Over time, however, the students themselves deviated from the scripted materials to identify topics they wanted to hear addressed. The Elders often spoke in Cree or Dene, which many students did not fully understand. The talks were translated and written down by

FIGURE 1

Spiral structure in original Generative Curriculum Model

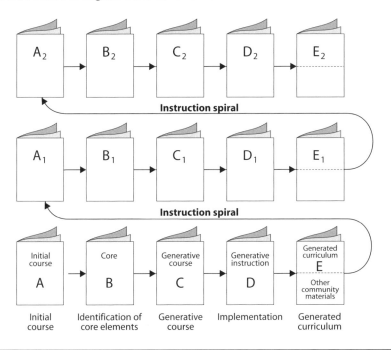

one of the instructors or a community member. After the program had been running for about a year, many of the Elders consented to having the sessions discreetly videotaped. The tapes formed the basis of a Tribal Council archive, "The Words of the Elders." The presentations were also transcribed into a Tribal Council publication, *The Elders Speak* (Greenwood et al. 1994).

The words of the Elders were initially understood as the principal generated component of the generative curriculum. However, as noted above, our understanding of "generative" has changed and expanded over time, forcing us to reconceptualize the initial framework used to describe the Generative Curriculum Model. As illustrated in Figure 1, the original model was a spiral structure. Each level of the spiral represents a multivoiced interaction, with the material generated at the previous iteration incorporated into successive course offerings. This approach to the Generative Curriculum Model has proven to be flawed, both pragmatically and conceptually.

In pragmatic terms, most of the relatively small First Nations communities that might use the Generative Curriculum Model were likely to train only one cohort of students every five or six years. It became increasingly clear that annual or successive intakes were unlikely. If successive intakes did occur, the students would probably be drawn from a much broader geographic area, requiring a regional rather than a community-based training approach. A regional approach could potentially result in the same type of pan-Aboriginal representations of knowledge that the Meadow Lake Tribal Council communities had rejected in their original search for First Nations ECCD curricula. Rather than risk diluting curriculum over time, we decided to continue to focus on more specific community partnerships.

The spiral representation has also proven to be conceptually flawed, as it reflects a linear process that moves from a less complete to a more complete curriculum over time. We now see the spiral model as a hybrid, incorporating modernist notions of knowledge refinement (content building) and post-modernist elements of content generation. While the former moves inexorably toward a state of completion, the latter has the potential to create a new and unique generation at each delivery – a living curriculum. In the original spiral model, the term "generative" had a strong sense of leading to an output, such as information generated by the community for the community's use. As the programs have evolved, "generative" has become ever more associated with the process rather than the products of generation. At the same time, the model itself has shifted from that of a spiral staircase, each step building on the one before, to a circular representation (Halldorson and Pence 1995) where each iteration represents a distinctive synthesis of participants and ideas (see Figure 2). The outcome of such a process can never be known in advance. Indeed, the outcome is multiple rather than singular and as diverse as the students, instructors, and community members who participate. Those multiple outcomes are themselves mutable, provisional, and transformational. Possibilities, not truth, emerge from the generative process.

As the Generative Curriculum Model has developed, the precise content of each training program is purposefully indeterminate to allow for culturally relevant and resonant co-construction of curriculum in each First Nations Partnership Program. No partnership starts with a blank slate, nor are instructors and students encouraged to adopt wholesale the scripted materials and resources we provide. Instead, they are encouraged to consider the written curriculum and go beyond it. Students, Elders, and instructors critique, contribute to, and reconceptualize it from their own cultural vantage points. As a result, each partnership yields a curriculum that is conceived through interaction among community members about their own culture and about the ideas presented in the course materials we provide. The process of co-constructing curriculum often has more value

FIGURE 2

Generative curriculum circle model

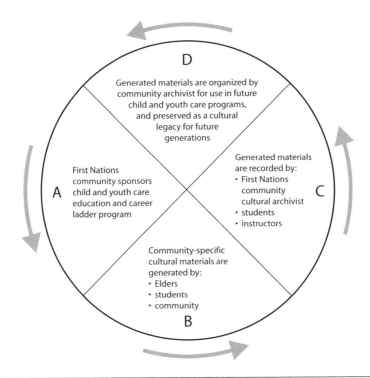

for a community than the final product itself. Nonetheless, that product – cultural knowledge that has been reconstructed and elaborated through the participatory process – is preserved for the community's use through audiotapes, videos, journals, and books.

The First Nations Partnership Programs' openness to "what will come" has posed a continual challenge in employing course developers and instructors. Much Western thought and action is based in predictability, in defining pre-established objectives and learning outcomes. Employing people who truly understand and appreciate the power of indeterminacy – of not knowing – has proven difficult. Many instructors and course developers envision an outcome, often one that challenges the status quo. In the Generative Curriculum Model, knowledge that challenges the status quo is a possible outcome. However, the outcome might also be consistent with an established conservative order – for example, support for the Catholic Church, a long-standing presence in several of the remote communities that have participated in the partnership programs. In the Generative Curriculum Model, the curriculum is dominated neither by the university's nor the community's contributions but is suspended in the space between – a space where disparate ideas can meet, combine, and transmogrify, with unforeseeable results.

Elders' Involvement and Cultural Healing

A long-term effect of colonization is that it steadily erodes the structures and practices of a healthy culture that allow community members to value their own and others' experiences as key events in an unfolding individual and collective life. Without those structures and practices, the content of knowledge, whether it originates from one's own or another's culture, has little resonance. Participants in the generative curriculum process experience themselves and others, often for the first time, as knowledgeable members of a community that is rich with power and potential. The interactive process that develops over time between students, Elders, instructors, and community members is at least as important as the generated Aboriginal content.

The Generative Curriculum Model fosters an environment in which cultural rejuvenation can take place. The involvement of Elders brings even the most disenchanted students into a circle of belonging to a healing cultural community. The Elders and other respected community members become conduits between the classroom and the community and, as participants in both worlds, they are part of the transformational process. This process has been particularly striking in communities that initially had difficulty envisioning how Elders' teachings might make a positive contribution to the child care training program. Members of some communities in the First Nations Partnership Programs expressed concerns such as the following:

> We have no healthy community members over fifty years old.

> Our old people all attended residential school and as a result they don't know the culture and have forgotten the language.

> The Elders here were all converted to Christianity and that is what they are likely to want to teach us.

While these community members were convinced that mainstream training programs would not be culturally sensitive or applicable to their communities, they initially were at a loss as to where community-specific traditional cultural input for the curriculum could come from. We also had doubts about whether a co-constructive process intended to embody elements of the traditional culture of the partner communities would be feasible in these cases. Initially, we held off commencing these programs until local Elder speakers could be identified. The communities were anxious to begin, however, and agreements were negotiated to bring in outside speakers, including First Nations speakers and Elders well known in the region. Eventually, students suggested inviting their elderly relatives. Before long, other Elders in the community offered workshops on traditional crafts, language, and ceremonies. In these communities, the Elders and their stories were essentially rediscovered by the students in the program.

For many participants, the child care training program is, in part, a journey of healing that enables them to reclaim their voices and reconnect to their culture. Elders played a major role in this rejuvenation. As one student notes,

> I learned from the Elders how to raise my daughter and how to forgive. We never got any teachings when we were young because we were in residential school. The Elders gave us their teaching and their words and helped us to become better parents. Learning communication skills also brought me closer to my daughter.

Louise Underwood, intergenerational facilitator in the Cowichan Tribes partnership, explains:

> The Elders have the soul for what we do. They give us their wisdom and their hope. In turn, they feel welcomed and respected, some of them for the first time. There is just so much love that goes around in this process. It's like a big circle.

Bridging the Generations

Even in a First Nations context, the passing of wisdom from one generation to another does not happen automatically. In the First Nations Partnership Programs, intergenerational facilitators play a pivotal role in enabling curriculum generation, promoting reinstatement of traditional teaching and learning roles, and stimulating social cohesion.[1] In most of

---

1 The importance of having a planned process and a designated individual to facilitate meetings between Elders and students and to support cultural learning was especially brought to light in a research investigation of the first seven partnerships, described in Chapter 7 (Ball 2000).

the partnership programs, the role of the intergenerational facilitator is filled by someone well situated to elicit the active involvement of a broad network of Elders to participate in the program. In two partnership programs, these individuals were Elders themselves and widely respected as knowledgeable about child care and development in their culture. The late Louis Opikokew, intergenerational facilitator in the Meadow Lake partnership, described his work with the Elders and its long-term repercussions in the community:

> I started by "sharing a few words" in the classes. Then I started inviting other Elders to come and talk about our culture. Many times we began with a pipe ceremony, but we always opened and closed with a prayer from the Elders. Both Cree and Dene Elders were equally involved in the program. There were times when Elders were hesitant to come. They had not been directly involved in Tribal Council programs before. I used to travel to their homes and explain to them what was expected. I asked them to tell their own story first and to just be themselves. Then I would tell them what topic was to be discussed, and asked them to think about it so they could say a few words about it in the class. Today we have Elders in all our programs at both the Tribal Council and First Nation levels. Whenever there is a conference we have a pipe ceremony at the start of each day ... We have finally recognized the wisdom and knowledge of our Cree and Dene Elders as a significant part of our life, and our work.

In addition to liaising with participating Elders and contributing knowledge themselves, intergenerational facilitators play an important role in helping some students – and, in some cases, instructors – to overcome their resistance to the unfamiliar practice of putting Indigenous knowledge at the core of curriculum development. Some students are receptive and welcome Elders as co-constructors of the curriculum, but others doubt that the "old ways" have any value or relevance to themselves, their families, or their future careers in child and youth care. The intergenerational facilitator needs to be especially adept at helping students tolerate ambiguities in the Elders' often indirect method of teaching through storytelling. As noted by Louise Underwood, intergenerational facilitator in the Cowichan Tribes partnership,

> When they first started, some of the students had difficulty staying still and really listening and hearing. But that is something that you develop, and this is part of our teaching ... The circle has been broken for so long, our ancestral

traditions have been put aside for so long, that the students need time, especially in the beginning. Time to recover who they are. Time to see that they are being asked and [have] been given an opportunity to inherit all the accumulated wisdom of all the generations of people in our Nation who have gone before them. Time to grow into being the leaders in our community that they will become.

The intergenerational facilitator also serves as a kind of socio-cultural informant for instructors from outside the community, introducing instructors and Elders to one another. The role of facilitating between generations might be an effective innovation in other community-inclusive training initiatives that seek to bridge the worlds of mainstream academe and Indigenous communities (Ball et al. 2002). The intergenerational facilitator's roles and responsibilities are summarized in Table 5.

Generating Curriculum in Community: Lil'wat Nation

Lil'wat Nation is located in the coastal mountains northeast of Vancouver, British Columbia. Its cultural roots were already well established at the outset of the partnership. Within this Nation, which represents five communities of Stl'atl'imx people, knowledge of their traditional language (Lil'wat) and customs continues to be passed down through a well-organized group of Elders. This Elder structure was easily adapted to the needs of the partnership program. In 1997, when the chief and band council shared their ideas for setting up an ECCD training program, they were committed to an educational process that Christine Leo, Director of Community Advancement Programs, Lil'wat Nation, aptly described as community development "from the inside out":

> We need our own community members to be leaders in the changes to come here. And when we get our daycare up and running, we need them to be staffing that service. We can't rely on outsiders to come in here. They won't know how to approach our families, what some of the things are that parents are facing. They won't know our Elders and what the Elders want to have happen here. And that's why we need this training program. So that we can do it ourselves, and we can do it our own way.

The university-based team collaborated with the band council, instructors, community Elders, and other local resource people for nearly two years to develop a training program built around the culture of the Stl'atl'imx people and the daily lives of children and families in Lil'wat Nation. Elders

TABLE 5

Roles and responsibilities of the intergenerational facilitator

Roles	Responsibilities
Plays a central role in this type of training program.	Seeks the participation of many Elders and other community members.
Is a bridge between the students and the Elders in their communities.	Helps students with the development of questions for Elders. Usually it works best when the questions ask for personal experiences, such as "What was your experience as a child in our community?"
Helps to make a bridge between what the students learn about caring for children and what their traditional culture tells them.	Encourages students to go to the Elders' homes when invited. In fact, sometimes Elders are more comfortable with home visits than with coming to class. Some Elders like to develop personal relationships with students through home visits. Home visits may solve transportation problems as well.
Helps to make sure there is good communication and a good feeling between the students, the instructors, and the Elders.	Helps, when necessary, with the English translation of traditional languages used by Elders.
Creates links among the students' home communities.	Arranges transportation for the Elders to come to class.
	Is sensitive to feelings that Elders may have about class participation and makes Elders feel welcome and appreciated.
	Follows appropriate customs, such as providing gifts to Elders as thanks for their participation.
	Encourages students to show respect for Elders.

and other community resource people met weekly with program participants to discuss and model traditional customs, language, and values related to children's stages of development. At the same time, instructors and students examined child development theories and curriculum approaches taught in mainstream ECCD training programs.

This participatory approach forged new relationships between generations. The dialogue that began in the classroom between the Elders and the students renewed respect in the community for the cultural knowledge and heritage preserved in the Elders' wisdom and generated pride in the people's First Nations identity. Marie Leo, a revered Lil'wat Elder who participated in the program, described her experience:

> I really enjoy it, going over there and answering questions that the students give us. It's really needed for the young people to remember our ways, how we raised our children and how we discipline them. And we talk about it in our language so that we can get it right.

A student in the program summarized her experience:

> This program is unique in giving me the chance to learn from my Elders what I need to know about who I am and my culture's ways of being with children. I couldn't learn this from any textbook, and I couldn't reach out to the children in my community ... without knowing what the Elders can teach me.

For Martina Pierre, one of three instructors recruited from within Lil'wat Nation, the training program responded to the community's goal of "reclaiming our heritage, our cultural traditions, rituals, and ceremonies." She added that students "wanted this experience so that as caregivers they will be more balanced in their lives, in their own self-concept and identity." Reclaiming a cultural heritage was especially significant for the generation of Lil'wat band members who had been taken away from their communities and confined in residential schools where their languages and cultural practices were prohibited and punished. Pierre explained: "When we began as new instructors, we began to rediscover ourselves. We looked at the things that were missing in our lives and said, 'This is what we want for our children.' So this program was very important."

In May of 1999, a multiplex with the Lil'wat name of *Pqusnalhcw*, or Eagle's Nest, opened on the Lil'wat Nation reserve. The multiplex houses the Lil'wat Health Centre and a thirty-two-space child care centre. The day before the official opening, the gymnasium reverberated with the thunder of drums as Lil'wat Nation honoured the fourteen graduates of the community-based, university-accredited program. It was a day to celebrate the old and new ways of the Stl'atl'imx people, as the children and families of Lil'wat Nation embarked on their future.

Reflections on the Generative Curriculum Model

If knowledge is more than a product, then it is not, in effect, something we possess but a mode of existence that allows our own experiences – of speaking, of listening – to emerge in the moment as significant events that contribute to a larger creative endeavour, the outcome of which cannot be known and in which our presence matters. It is this experience that ultimately confers upon knowledge its power, and the experience is strengthened when we share it with others.

The Generative Curriculum Model embodies the principle that useful knowledge exists only in interaction, in praxis. Such knowledge is mutable and takes its form from the environment in which it was created. Like water, it is endlessly transforming. The act of co-construction requires a level of trust and sharing seldom found and not required in knowledge-transfer approaches that seek to fill one mind from another. To understand knowledge as a commodity that can be bought and traded without engendering personal commitment and sharing is to ignore the heart of learning and to lose the affective power within which transformational learning resides. Knowledge accumulation without transformation is a sterile process that permits one only to accumulate wealth, but not to create it. Such distinctions are critical if we are to move beyond the limited vision of modernity.

For those who work across cultures, the singularity and immutability of the modernist agenda have always been problematic. Creating space to explore the idea of multiple truths, however – and allowing these truths to mix in order to see what might emerge from their interaction – has not occurred in the practice of most educational and social services, including the world of ECCD. At the same time, the history of introducing scientifically "proven" program transplants into dissimilar contexts has not resulted in healthy sustainability. The First Nations Partnership Programs can be seen as a practical response to a social and educational dilemma. By collaborating in a true and open partnership to co-construct curriculum from the inside out, the hopes, visions, and responsibilities of First Nations and their institutional partners can be realized.

Sitting Backwards at Our Desks

I hope you people at the university are learning as much from us as we are learning from you. It's important for university lecturers and theorists to listen and learn ... what being Indian means.
　　　– Judy Maas, former chief, Treaty 8 Tribal Association

Teachers as Learners, Learners as Teachers

Post-secondary education reflects and engenders the culturally conditioned values and practices of those who design and deliver the curricula. This is especially evident in the social sciences, in teacher training, and in other human services training. Many educators around the globe, especially outside North America, have expressed concern about the lack of representation of non-Western values, content, and methods at all levels of education (Battiste and Barman 1995; Ki-Zerbo et al. 1997; Smith 1999). There is growing concern among observers of international education and exchange projects in the Majority World about the harm that has been done by ethnocentric curriculum and programs of research and technical assistance presided over by Western educators (Ball 1998; Dahlberg, Moss, and Pence 1999; Ki-Zerbo et al. 1997; Shiva 1997). This critique extends to the cultural holocaust caused by imposing Western best practices on the traditional cultures, languages, and communities of North America's Indigenous peoples (Battiste and Barman 1995; Taylor, Crago, and McAlpine 1993).

Our experiences with the First Nations Partnership Programs confirm that a participatory approach holds the most promise for furthering an anti-colonial agenda. We believe that the Generative Curriculum Model has promising applications in community- and institution-based education and training in North America and beyond, particularly in the human services, and particularly when working with diverse cultural and ethnic groups.

Research has taught us the importance at all levels of student-centred teaching strategies that promote active learning rather than passive receipt of provided knowledge (Ball 1994). True engagement in learning requires two things: a relevant and meaningful curriculum that affirms students' identities and experiences; and classroom processes that empower students to be self-directed (Freire 1970/1993; Giroux 1992; Lockhart 1982).

A glimpse into the history of teacher training in North America reveals that teachers have traditionally been trained to be the bearers and disseminators of knowledge. Little emphasis has been placed on engaging students in an interactive process of teaching and learning. And, in most mainstream programs, teacher training has fallen short of preparing teachers to reflect on their own assumptions and beliefs and how these affect their work with students.

For the most part, teachers are trained in a linear and sequential manner that is characteristic of Western culture but not well suited to learners from other cultures (Stahl 1992). A major downfall of most mainstream teacher training is an emphasis on the logical steps through which a teacher proceeds rather than on the way students actually think, learn, and are motivated to pay attention. Typically, teachers are trained toward action and breadth and not toward reflection and depth in teaching; Brookfield (1991) argues that this focus leaves students feeling that they never really have the necessary opportunities to allow them to master skills or new knowledge adequately. Bowman (1994) points out that teachers are seldom encouraged to find out about the history, resources, beliefs, and values of their students' cultures. Moreover, teachers are rarely helped to understand how and why students' learning styles may differ from their own.

Numerous authors in education fields have written about the components of effective teaching. Together, they highlight three areas that are underemphasized in most teacher training programs: the importance of reflection in practice; the inclusion of students' knowledge and experience as valued sources of knowledge; and the development of interpersonal relationships with students.

Stahl (1992) and others argue that to work effectively with students, teachers need to change the way they perceive themselves as teachers and attend to knowing how they are embedded in their own culture. According to Bowman (1994), "Teachers must draw on and face their own backgrounds, empathies and cultural preferences and prejudices in order to know themselves as well as their children."

Robertson (1996) differentiates between simple and transformative learning: in simple learning more content is learned, but the basic structure of the learner's perspective is preserved; in transformative learning, the learner's paradigm contains the old one but, rather than being an elaboration, it becomes a new creation. Teachers who see their role as that of disseminating knowledge will remain aloof and their students' learning will be simple in form; conversely, teachers who see themselves as facilitators of learning will engage their students in intimate relationships, engendering learning that transforms both their students and themselves (Robertson 1996).

Becker and Varelas (1995) believe that a teacher's role is to assist learners to construct knowledge, thus it is important to consider how the teacher's pre-existing knowledge influences the learner's construction of new knowledge. It is vital that teachers present themselves authentically (Wilson 1994). In research on factors that facilitate performance and achievement among minority students, Wilson (1994) found that First Nations students wanted to learn from faculty who showed their own humanity and made students feel cared about and important. In "Aboriginal Epistemology," Ermine (1995) stresses the importance of integrating subjective experiences and introspection into learning processes. He proposes that learning that reaffirms first language and culture has the potential to transform. In his words, "Experience is knowledge" (1995, 109).

In describing the process of learning that enables individuals to operate within a culture different from their own, Taylor (1994) builds on Mezirow's theory of perspective transformation and extends it to emphasize the role of critical reflection. His model enumerates the skills required of teachers who want to work effectively with students of diverse populations. Quoting Mezirow, Taylor defines reflection as a "deliberate assessment of the justification for our beliefs, ideas, and feelings" (1994, 170). Persons with a reflective orientation engage in deep critical thought about becoming interculturally competent and increase the likelihood that they will be able to operate effectively within a culture that is different from their own.

All of these components of effective teaching have been essential to the teaching and learning processes employed in the Generative Curriculum Model.

A Community of Learners

An attribute of the Generative Curriculum Model is that learning occurs all ways, with instructors and university-based partners positioned to learn as much as the students and community-based partners in program delivery. Throughout the program planning and delivery, instructors are exposed to different experiences and viewpoints, and are often challenged and stimulated by them. Students, hearing the diverse voices and views of Elders, other community members, instructors, and classmates, become more aware of their own voices, their views, and how these relate to the views of others. Together, in a "community of learners" (Rogoff 1994), all become engaged in an ongoing process of learning and teaching.

In the Generative Curriculum Model, instructors promote active learning by structuring high levels of student involvement. Students are asked to contribute their experience and ideas, critique the provided curriculum materials, gather and discuss information from local sources, and gather new data. Ultimately, they are asked to construct concepts and practice models informed by this generated curriculum. Instructors increase the personal relevance and social applicability of what is taught by recruiting knowledgeable and respected members of students' communities to generate curriculum content and learning activities and to play an active role in teaching. Students ask community members both pre-planned and spontaneous questions about their academic subject matter. At the same time, instructors structure individual and small-group learning activities and assignments that engage students with mainstream textbooks and course manuals representing established Western knowledge on the subject. Instructors facilitate the evolution of a community of learners in which students, community members, and the instructor engage in critical discussion, debate, expansion, and application of the Indigenous and the university-based curriculum content. This approach has resulted in profound transformations for both teachers and learners who have participated in the First Nations Partnership Programs – indeed, our research study of the first seven partnership programs shed much light on the transformative impacts upon the instructors of teaching using the Generative Curriculum Model (Ball 2000).

The Generative Curriculum Model places special demands on instructors. Generative curriculum development proceeds from the assumption that all participants in the generative process have valuable knowledge to contribute. Inviting community members to collaborate in co-constructing curricula and placing culturally embedded concepts at the core instead of the periphery of education has profound implications for educators. This approach affects the kinds of questions we ask about the roles of teachers and students as agents of learning, cultural articulation, and social development.

Many instructors in the First Nations Partnership Programs have never co-constructed curriculum before. For them, the experience of putting the knowledge and experience of students and community members at the forefront of class discussions is new. It is also the first time many have truly experienced working with cultural differences and facilitating an atmosphere of learning grounded in the life of a community – all critical components of teaching within the Generative Curriculum Model. Most instructors find their first experience of teaching within the model challenging. Facilitating the co-construction of a curriculum that considers many perspectives can be unsettling at first. As one instructor from the Meadow Lake Tribal Council said, "When the classes started ... I felt like an experienced 'rookie.' I had never taught generatively before and I felt like I was sitting backwards in my desk."

Co-Constructing/Co-Instructing the Generative Curriculum

Each course in the Generative Curriculum Model is designed to be taught generatively. Instructors using the generative approach do far more than explore ideas from textbooks with their students. They also elicit from students and Elders the perspectives of their own First Nations community on the topics being studied. The instructor's task is to present the assumptions, approaches, and research findings reported in the textbooks and to help students view this material from their community's point of view. Instructors in the First Nations Partnership Programs co-instruct with Elders and other respected community members. Instructors need to be responsive to input from Elders, and this means responsive not just to the knowledge they share but also to their ways of doing things. In the Meadow Lake program, for example,

it started out that the Elders sat at the front of the class and all the students were at their tables and they kind of chatted to us from up there. The students took notes and it was very much like a classroom situation and ... it came from the Elders that "This isn't the way we do this ... We don't talk this way. It's disrespectful while we're speaking for our peoples' heads to be down like this and writing. We talk in a circle. There's all these tables between us and there's no interaction, there's no real connection happening there" ... [It] was kind of a turning point ... It became more of a sharing kind of situation. (Instructor, Meadow Lake Tribal Council)

Teaching generatively requires instructors to help students make connections in the space between the emergent Indigenous curriculum and the scripted university-based curriculum:

Quite often the students would feel like what the Elder said had contradicted something I had been teaching. So, then it was up to me to put it all together on my feet. You really had to be listening in the Elder's session and be thinking as you went, anticipating what this is going to turn into by the next morning. I needed to be ready for my class because those would be the moments when you could really help students to make the connections and comparisons between the Indigenous knowledge and the research-based knowledge. (Instructor, Meadow Lake Tribal Council)

Valuing Students' Knowledge and Experience

Most instructors are new to the process of putting the knowledge and experience of students, Elders, and other community members at the forefront of class discussions. Within the Generative Curriculum Model, instructors do not sift, censor, evaluate, or attempt to modify knowledge contributed by students and community contributors. To teach generatively, instructors need to be open to realities that differ from their own and to value their students' knowledge and experience:

I spent the first three months learning how to listen, how to provide a culture of trust – a safe place where students could learn new information and assess the perceived value of that information in the context of their life experiences ... As an instructor, I, too, felt empowered by this process. (Instructor, Cowichan Tribes)

Knowledge presented in glossy textbooks is often intimidating for First Nations students and community members. Like students in most classrooms (but with the added dimension of cultural distance), they have been conditioned to feel that their words could never be as worthy as those, printed on the page, of "experts" imported from outside the cultural community. Consequently, instructors must make an explicit effort to lead with the local knowledge:

I've always thought of adult learners as being contributors, but never really as being contributors first – first asking them what they know and then going to the textbook or whatever the material was. (Instructor, Meadow Lake Tribal Council)

With the Indigenous way of learning, you always try to go from local to national to international. It was important for the students first to know about the topics from an Indigenous viewpoint, and then learn about national policies and programs, and then learn about international programs of research, theories, and practice models. (Instructor, Nzen'man' Child and Family Services)

Rather than emphasize their own beliefs and perspectives in the classroom, instructors facilitate discussion of various perspectives and sources of knowledge:

> What I wanted for human services as an instructor was probably less important than what the Elders and other members of the students' own communities were saying to them and what their own ideas were. We integrated all those ideas. We didn't all envision the same things, but they were all valuable things for them to consider in becoming effective human services workers. (Instructor, Meadow Lake Tribal Council)

Working with Cultural Differences

Instructors in some of the First Nations Partnership Programs have been non-Aboriginal, their expertise rooted in another culture. For instructors who are not of First Nations descent, learning to recognize and accept the differences between Aboriginal and non-Aboriginal styles of communication and interaction is critical. Much of instructors' success in working with cultural differences rests on their ability to understand the assumptions and beliefs of their own cultures:

> I come from a culture where being able to speak quickly and being able to respond [quickly] and be eloquent is a very highly prized commodity ... [I am] beginning to understand ... [and] appreciate the different ways of expressing. You shouldn't go around making assumptions about people based on how quickly they answer or how complicated their sentences are when they do answer. (Instructor, Meadow Lake Tribal Council)

> In a [mainstream] classroom, we were raised to say, "Oh, I know that," and put up our hand, to stand out and show your knowledge and demonstrate your worth. In First Nations communities, that is not necessarily a valued thing. (Instructor, Cowichan Tribes)

> Silence is really intimidating to us in our [non-Aboriginal] culture. It's not something that generally I think we feel very comfortable with, and I think that one of the major [lessons] for me was that ability now to actually be silent and let the silence fall. (Instructor, Cowichan Tribes)

I learned that with First Nations students it was not okay to single people out, either as examples of something really good or something really not so good. (Instructor, Cowichan Tribes)

In the First Nations Partnership Programs, non-Indigenous instructors do not attempt to become experts in Indigenous ways of knowing:

A non-First Nations instructor can never really know what the experiences of the students have been like, or the experience of living in the community – you can visit, you can work there every day and still not have awareness of many things. It is really important to be aware of not knowing and open to learning from the students. (Instructor, Tl'azt'en Nation)

Grounding Learning in Experience

Providing information and knowledge cannot by itself produce the breadth of learning that the generative approach makes possible. The "community of learners" approach advocated by Rogoff (1994) emphasizes the importance of social context in education. In addition, historical experiences with school, literacy, and traditional language need to be part of the educational context. This approach may be particularly important in working with ethnically or culturally marginalized groups, where traditional sources of knowledge have been devalued.

For students to truly learn, coursework must be relevant to their lives. In the First Nations Partnership Programs, the process of learning is grounded in the community:

Knowledge, as I have experienced it, is often derived from outside myself; that is, information is objectified, logical, and provable. Listening to the Elders and other community members, knowledge for them appears to be generated from within oneself, and set within the context of their reality. (Instructor, Meadow Lake Tribal Council)

The Generative Curriculum Model calls for instructors and students to ground learning in students' experiences as members of their cultural communities, and students become invested in their education as a process of illuminating their lives and preparing for their own new roles in service to their communities:

It slowly starts to sink in and then you understand. So, when you talk about teaching the medicine wheel, well, the medicine wheel is a concept, it's a picture on a page. When the Elders start speaking of their beliefs in whole terms, then it becomes something I can sort of attach to. Much the same way as [I felt about] the pipe ceremony: sitting on the outside of the circle looking in is not like being in a circle at all. (Instructor, Meadow Lake Tribal Council)

Instructor Transformations

When instructors engage in reflection, consider other perspectives, value the knowledge and experience of students and Elders, and integrate these into their work, the experience is transformative. This student describes the changes she observed in her instructors over the duration of the program:

> My instructors over the two years were phenomenal. It was so funny to see them change. They had these rigid boundaries at first. It was like, "I'm your teacher, you're my student." And by the time the program was over, they'd learned as much from us as we did from them. Before, it was the professional appearance and we were divided by the desks. By the end of the program we were like friends. And it was good to have that connection with them, because you know they are people too and you can approach them or say things to them or tell them anything. (Student, Nzen'man' Child and Family Services)

Instructors in the First Nations Partnership Programs typically find that they become more open, reflective, and responsive in their teaching styles:

> The key thing that improved me as an instructor was I learned to wait. I learned to not expect immediate answers, immediate feedback, and [I learned] to give things a chance, wait for the relevance to emerge. Sometimes people would say something that didn't seem relevant to the discussion and then I would figure out later on that it was really relevant and that the other students could quite often see this relevance. I learned to look for messages in different ways, too. Sometimes students would use humour to give me a message that something was not relevant for them or to their culture. (Instructor, Cowichan Tribes)

Many instructors become more aware of their own cultural values and traditions – a development they often do not anticipate. One instructor recounts that while she was prepared to ask students to explore their culture, roots, and family connections, she was taken aback when they asked her to do the same. However, the result was personally transforming:

It really forced me to dig around and think about what I did learn from my ancestors and why it was important to me and whether I still value it or not. It's a really interesting personal exploration exercise. (Instructor, Cowichan Tribes)

Student Transformations

Students in the First Nations Partnership Programs experience an increased sense of cultural identity, self-esteem, parenting effectiveness, and confidence as community leaders. Instructors and students alike provide eloquent testimony to such transformations:

There was a lot more sharing as the course went on, because people became more confident, they found a voice for themselves. I really remember the women coming into my classroom. They would speak with their heads down and in a voice so quiet that you couldn't hear it. And now I can honestly say that every single student can speak out and say what she needs to say. (Instructor, Tl'azt'en Nation)

One of the things that really struck me ... is the ability of the students to think analytically and critically. Not only did their academic skills, in terms of their reading and their writing and their confidence, increase but they also became so willing to pick things apart. And what we hear now from the students who are at a fourth-year level [in a non-generative environment, is that] ... they were influencing the mainstream classroom to start also picking things apart. I just think that we challenged them so much to think about theory in terms of its relevance to their own communities that they became so skilled. (Instructor, Cowichan Tribes)

The program made me discover the things that I was capable of doing, the things that I didn't know I had, the skills which came about in doing the coursework, and the things that we did with the children in my practicum experiences. (Student, Onion Lake First Nation)

The First Nations Partnership Programs have higher rates of student completion than those reported for First Nations students in other post-secondary programs in Canada. Graduates of the First Nations Partnership Programs have also demonstrated a much greater commitment to remain in their communities to work. The Generative Curriculum Model's focus on community highlights for students their potential to contribute to the health and well-being of their communities:

People are really optimistic about having this future employment in ECE – a lot of hope – the need for placing that significant value on the language, culture, and traditions ... helps the esteem, validating the worth of those things ... because they had, for many historical reasons, been undervalued, undermined. (Instructor, Lil'wat Nation)

When students talk about the ideal child care centre, they bring a lot of the traditions into their ideas about programming. (Instructor, Treaty 8 Tribal Association)

The program has given me the strength and caring for the community ... I really believe that I am a role model for the kids. (Student, Cowichan Tribes)

We're the ones who are going to make the big change in our communities. (Student, Lil'wat Nation)

The Generative Curriculum Model gives Indigenous students and instructors an opportunity to unlearn some of the negative self-concepts that have developed over decades of being subjected to practices aimed at eradicating Indigenous culture and language:

It's a self-healing program. A lot of looking back. From my point of view, we have had to put a lot of things on the shelf in our personal life. We didn't deal with them. Now, with this program, we have to look at ourselves. And it's pretty upsetting sometimes, when you think back ... That is positive because we all have to deal with our lives sooner or later and this is ... a way of healing ourselves. (Instructor, Lil'wat Nation)

Almost all [the students] have a certain change in how they feel about themselves ... This course does bring them back to childhood and they have to deal with it. It's almost like a healing while they are taking the training at the same time. (Instructor, Lil'wat Nation)

Attributes of Effective Teachers

We believe that to teach effectively within the Generative Curriculum Model instructors need to possess a number of personal characteristics and be committed to specific actions. These are summarized in Table 6.

The personal attributes described in Table 6 foster fundamentally different teaching methods from those that typically occur in a mainstream classroom. During the evaluation of the First Nations Partnership Programs,

TABLE 6

Instructor characteristics and actions

Personal characteristics	Actions
Open	▪ Listen
	▪ Acknowledge contributions of others
	▪ Express valuing others
Self-aware	▪ Practise reflection
	▪ Strive to learn about others
	▪ Encourage feedback
Values relationship	▪ Present self authentically
	▪ Trust others
	▪ Share personal information
	▪ Express feelings
	▪ Demonstrate caring and concern for others

nineteen instructors who had taught in the programs underscored how their teaching had differed in fundamental ways from prevailing teaching approaches in universities and professional training programs. To capture these differences, the instructors were asked to formulate advice for instructors who would use the Generative Curriculum Model in the future. Their advice, based on their reflections of what they had found effective in their teaching practices in the partnership programs, included:

▪ Respect the cultural and historical experience of community members as valuable sources of knowledge, rather than elevating the authority of Euro-Western theories and research on child and youth care and development.
▪ Assert the power of not knowing where an informed discussion might lead, rather than maintaining the colonialist presumption of knowing what's best for all people.
▪ Ground teaching and learning in a consideration of many voices, rather than relying on the modernist approach of universal truths and best practices for children and families.
▪ Encourage participatory processes at every stage of program design and delivery, rather than offering prepackaged curricula developed by "experts."

■ Work consciously to promote social inclusion in capacity building, rather than accepting the exclusivity that has often been imposed by professional gatekeeping organizations and by dominant cultures.

■ Be prepared to join in a community of learners as an authentic participant, and be receptive to being transformed as thoroughly as are the students.

Reflections on Teaching and Learning

Throughout the delivery and evaluation of the First Nations Partnership Programs, we have discovered that the Generative Curriculum Model embodies many principles that others in education have argued are important. Allman et al. (1998) and Ermine (1995), among others, have been proponents of the wealth of experience and knowledge that students bring to the learning group. To benefit from this source of knowledge, educators must be willing and able to cross the boundaries that have framed their present experience, a process that requires them to develop awareness and understanding of the impact their own beliefs and assumptions may have in the classroom. This process engenders a reliance on self-knowledge that enables both students and teachers to be effective learners.

To establish trust and engage in practice that highlights the contributions of others, teachers must look within, drawing on their own backgrounds, empathies, cultural preferences, and prejudices (Bowman 1994, 224). Empowerment flows from approaches that allow students to have a voice: "In the specific case of empowerment through educational action ... the process is one that transforms the people who have the formal knowledge and the people who are acquiring formal knowledge" (Lima and Gazzetta 1994, 237).

The relationships that develop between instructors and students are an important part of an effective learning experience. Students in the First Nations Partnership Programs often echoed the words of Peggy Wilson's Aboriginal students, who valued accessible, approachable, available instructors (Wilson 1994). These students experienced learning as inextricable from the emotional realm of caring and chose to engage in learning only with instructors they saw as genuine. Brookfield (1991) agrees that an atmosphere of trust is important in the classroom. Such an atmosphere is facilitated by teachers who present themselves as whole people and who demonstrate congruency between their words and actions.

Consistent with our experience with the Generative Curriculum Model, Robertson (1996) suggests that when teachers adopt a reflective stance and value students' knowledge and experience in the educational process, the transformative learning process necessarily affects both teachers and learners. Transformative learning occurs within an educational helping relationship in which teachers are facilitators of learning rather than disseminators of knowledge.

The Generative Curriculum Model has many potential applications for teaching and learning in the human services, both in mainstream and community-based settings. It is especially valuable in work in cross-cultural contexts. Participatory teaching practices that encompass the broader social community can create new communities of learners who are encouraged to study and evaluate various sources of knowledge and their potential applicability in local contexts. Communities of learners can also create new knowledge that is culturally and contextually appropriate. Students can experience a high degree of agency in determining what they learn and how they learn it. Their education can reflect the settings in which they live and intend to work.

The words of Dennis Esperanz, an Indigenous educator and key liaison with one of our partner institutions, Saskatchewan Indian Institute of Technologies, underscore the value of reciprocal learning, not only in classrooms but between institutional and community partners:

> We educators have to be visionaries, but when we talk curriculum, we also have to consider the vision of people in our communities – what their goals are. The Generative Curriculum Model contains a larger vision of how to bring the two different visions together – the one that academics see and the one that guides people out there in the communities. So we've learned a new approach to making what we do here [in this institution] meaningful and effective for all parties. People are just starting to understand what this is all about.

Institutions and educators who work in cultural communities have as much to learn from their community partners as the communities have to learn from the institutions. Reciprocal learning depends on our willingness to look both ways, on "sitting backwards at our desks" to reposition ourselves with respect to our beliefs about where knowledge resides. From this new vantage point, we can explore the cultural contexts that give knowledge meaning and relevance. Communities are the proving grounds where ideas and approaches to child and family well-being are tested. In communities of learners, learning occurs "all ways."

Grounding Learning in the Heart of Communities

> We wanted a partner who was prepared to undertake a new relationship and look at curriculum in a new way that integrates First Nations culture, beliefs, and values into the heart of the curriculum, not just take existing off-the-shelf curriculum and modify it around the edges. We wanted something that really breathed the heart and soul of the communities.
>
> – Vern Bachiu, administrator, Meadow Lake Tribal Council

The Power of Community

One of the greatest challenges we all face is understanding where we are situated – in relation to where we live, in relation to the past and the future, and in relation to ourselves and members of our immediate and extended communities. Our context profoundly shapes the nature of any understandings we reach. Consider the following passage from Descartes' *Discourse on Method*:

> There was no conversation to occupy me, and being untroubled by any cares or passions, I remained all day alone in a warm room. There I had plenty of leisure to examine my ideas ... I concluded that I was a thing or substance whose whole essence or nature was only to think, and which, to exist, has no need of space nor of any material thing or body. (Descartes 1637/1960, 10:25)

It is hardly surprising that a man cogitating alone in a room, undisturbed by the challenges of relationships with other people and his wider surroundings, should conclude that he is essentially a disembodied thinker.

What is more surprising is that such a stance has been idealized within Western culture as a mark of intellectual refinement and, more critically, as a method of improving the human condition. The Cartesian tradition, upon which Western epistemology rests, holds that the ideal way to discover the truth is to isolate oneself from one's community so as to develop a supposedly objective stance from which to evaluate cultural teachings and traditions. What one learns from this stance can then be applied to everyday situations as part of an overall project of human progress. Few of us live within a strict version of this tradition, and although such ideals have been widely questioned within our culture, their influence is pervasive.

Leaving home – literally or figuratively – is a major rite of passage in the West. Intellectual maturity is often reached at the price of alienation from the teachings of one's childhood and youth. The maturation process frequently occurs in concert with a move from a hometown to a larger, more cosmopolitan centre, where traditional kinship ties are loose or nonexistent. Often this move occurs in conjunction with the pursuit of "higher learning," which usually takes place in an institution in a circumscribed location that is removed from the community in body and spirit. Generally, Western culture tends to regard development from childhood through to adulthood as a series of movements away from one's roots. We marvel at how far a person has come, and we tend to consider those who have remained close to home as having avoided life's greater challenges, as having somehow failed to reach their full potential.

It is perfectly possible, however, to view maturity as an ever deepening relationship with one's roots, as an evolving understanding of whom and where we have always been in relation to our ancestors, our traditions, and the place we live. This alternate view of development promotes the cultivation of wisdom rather than the accumulation of knowledge. Knowledge and wisdom both are necessary to the development of human potential. Western culture, however, tends to respond to every challenge as if what is inevitably needed is more knowledge – a commodity that often requires going farther afield – when what is wanted may be greater wisdom – a state that sometimes is reached by remaining where one is and patiently waiting for understanding to emerge from the situation.

Indigenous people in Canada are not alone in wishing to improve conditions for the children, youth, and families in their communities. The legacy of colonization, however, has left many First Nations communities with a particularly urgent need to foster conditions in which their people can thrive, both socially and economically. Post-secondary education is often viewed as a means to achieving this goal. But mainstream Western education has failed to strengthen communities in meaningful ways. Most First Nations students who leave their communities to pursue education and training find little that is relevant to their lives. As noted earlier, few complete their education. Those who do succeed in mainstream educational settings tend not to return home, resulting in incalculable losses to their communities. A typical mainstream response to this situation is to assume that to improve support for First Nations students, we need to apply more knowledge. On the basis of our experience with the Generative Curriculum Model, however, we would argue that a better alternative is to start from the assumption that First Nations people already have the capacity to strengthen conditions for children, youth, and families within their communities, and that what is required are supports that will allow this capacity to emerge and express itself in its own way and in its own time. One such support is post-secondary education and training that is truly community based.

The Generative Curriculum Model illustrates the power of the community not only to shape the learning experience but also to serve as its starting point or foundation. The First Nations Partnership Programs have all been delivered at the community level. This approach makes post-secondary education accessible to many people who otherwise might not participate or succeed in mainstream settings. The community location does more than make post-secondary education physically accessible, though. It incorporates the community into the very substance of the training program, resulting in a positive, transformative experience for program participants, community members, and the wider socio-cultural ecosystem.

We have concluded that even the best institution-based, mainstream post-secondary education could not achieve the same results. Community-based delivery enables extensive community involvement and other program processes that combine to distinguish the Generative Curriculum Model from what is generally recognized as good, constructivist, participatory pedagogy. Instructors at mainstream campuses who have compared the model to their own teaching experiences point to the difficulty of working with generative curriculum in programs where students are at a distance from their home communities. When the community is excluded from participating in capacity-building initiatives, the potential for community-wide transformations that could sustain and magnify the built capacity is seriously attenuated.

The Generative Curriculum Model also brings into focus a comparative view of varying educational terrains. The absence of community in mainstream university education, and the exclusion of community even in some programs that are located in the community, create major challenges for making professional training relevant. Students neither practice with nor receive feedback from the people they are training to serve. In the First Nations Partnership Programs, many graduates experience positive impacts on their own parenting because they do not need to leave their families to participate in the program; this enables ongoing opportunities for practice, feedback, and reflection on their child care practices in family and community contexts. The community-based program delivery generates links that enable community inclusion in the education process and that lead to community-wide ripple effects. When the community is given entry into the education process and invited to play meaningful roles, the benefits of the training do not end inside the classroom. Instead, community members carry the training program with them into the broad ecology of children's lives.

An Ecological Systems Model

An ecological systems model (Bronfenbrenner 1979) is useful to characterize the interactive context in which the training program emerges and which it impacts in turn.

FIGURE 3

The ecology of interacting elements in the First Nations Partnership training program

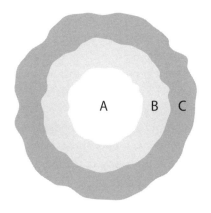

A **Microsystem:**
   students, instructors, and Elders
   curriculum input, university-based
   curriculum input, community-based
   administrators

B **Exosystem:**
   practicum supervisors
   staff
   children

C **Macrosystem:**
   inter-community,
   inter-agency, and
   broad interpersonal
   relationships

The inner circle depicted in Figure 3 represents the microsystem of participants directly involved in the training program – students, instructors, Elders, and university- and community-based administrators. The circle reverberating farther from the centre represents the exosystem, which includes structures within the First Nations community, within neighbouring communities that provide practicum opportunities, and within the partnering post-secondary institutions. Finally, the circle farthest from the centre represents the macrosystem, which includes the multicultural milieu of professional organizations, inter-agency structures, regional and federal funding policies and programs, and the socio-political position and status of First Nations individuals and communities within a broad societal matrix. In the First Nations Partnership Programs, high levels of engagement occur at all three levels.

Three major types of engagement are common at the microsystem level. A high level of interaction occurs among the participants, primarily involving dialogue about course content and learning assignments, but also involving mutual support for personal and academic challenges. A second type of interaction involves individual reflection and journal writing about the meanings of childhood in the home community and about goals for community initiatives aimed at supporting the development of children and families. Finally, participants are engaged in practical action in relationships with young children in students' families and in the community as a whole.

Ongoing mutual engagement occurs at the exosystem level between training program participants and individuals representing various supporting social-organizational structures. These interactions tend to focus on practical arrangements for sustaining the training program and on plans for implementing new programs for children and families. Participants' accounts of these interactions point to their recursive effects: changing and clarifying roles for people and organizations within the community and enhancing social cohesion.

Finally, at the level of the macrosystem, the program's ripple effects strengthen First Nations labour force participation, professional membership, and social acceptance, and also increase awareness among non-Indigenous people about Indigenous people's capabilities and distinctive characteristics with regard to child care and development. Following are examples at the micro-, exo-, and macro-levels of the positive potential of community-based education, as well as key features and challenges associated with this method of delivering training programs.

Developing Models of Culturally Appropriate Child Care

Because the Generative Curriculum Model encourages a high degree of reflection and interaction, students explore diverse possibilities for interpreting the meanings and practical implications of "development" and "quality care" in the context of their own culture and community and with reference to their own experiences as children and as caregivers. Guidelines for culturally desirable child care practices emerge through in-class dialogue about the cultural reconstructions and experiences elaborated by Elders in the community, contemporary social conditions and local goals for children, and ideas and research found in mainstream texts and practicum observations. It is unlikely that this dialogue could occur or bear fruit in the absence of community-based delivery.

An example of a new construction of culturally fitting, community-appropriate practice is found in one partnership program that brings children and caregivers together in a talking circle when a child engages in challenging behaviours in the child care centre. A salient feature of most Indigenous cultures in Canada is the extensive use of stories, rather than direct instruction or explicit feedback, as the preferred way of teaching children about their community's norms, moral values, and behavioural expectations. During the talking circles, stories are told that imply the need for children to cooperate, demonstrate self-control, and defer to the authority of the Elders. A student explains:

> We don't usually think of using "time out" with a child who is not doing what we want him to do. To many of us here, isolating the child from his community seems to be the opposite of what we want him to learn. Maybe the child needs to be brought in even closer within the circle of his community, and to hear talk from his friends about what they are trying to accomplish. Then he might see how he is needed to help the group ... We need to stay in close touch with a child who is not doing what we have asked him to do so that we can get a better understanding of his spirit – of who he is and what he is needing. Stories can be used to speak to the spirit of that child. More than anything else we need to be patient with him. (Student, Lil'wat Nation)

In familiar surroundings, students actively engage in an ongoing process of articulating, comparing, and integrating Euro-Western and Indigenous knowledge in their teaching practices. For example, after Elders in one partnership program discussed the tradition of the cradle board (a decorated board designed to hold a swaddled infant), we observed children being wrapped in beaded cradle boards and placed in cribs. After nap time, the cradle boards were placed near where the children were crawling and climbing. The cradle board became both a functional and a visual object within the environment, bringing together old and new traditions. Familiar and culturally relevant environments are maintained and sometimes transformed as students gain a new awareness of the ways in which they, as professional educators, affect children's emotional, physical, social, and cognitive development.

Community Transformations

One of the most striking benefits of locating the training program in the community is the opportunity for community participation in post-secondary education. Widespread benefits flow both ways: from the community to the students and from the students to the community. The First Nations Partnership Programs create widespread effects at the community level, these benefits being most obvious in communities that start out with a strong foundation of social cohesion on which to build. For example, the partnership with Tl'azt'en Nation illustrates the potential for community-based and generated post-secondary education to effect transformations in communities that start out with less social cohesion. The partnership with Treaty 8 Tribal Association highlights the importance of the community base in influencing the extent to which community benefits can flow from the Generative Curriculum Model.

Tl'azt'en Nation Partnership

Tl'azt'en Nation consists of about eight hundred Carrier people spread across three villages north of the remote outpost of Fort St. James in northern British Columbia. When administrators from the Nation contacted us in 1996 to explore the possibility of entering into a partnership to deliver a child care training program, they expressed doubts about the community's capacity to implement the Generative Curriculum Model. They did not believe that many of the community's Elders would be able to participate in generating curriculum, and they were skeptical of the value of the Elders' potential contributions to the program. In initial meetings with community members, we ourselves had serious doubts about whether the Generative Curriculum Model could be implemented successfully in this community, given that Elders were not active in community life at that time. However, the partnership was struck, and the program let to evolve according to the pace dictated by community needs and interests. We were then privileged to witness a profound transformation in the Tl'azt'en Nation as a whole – a transformation that was all the more remarkable because the odds against the program's success had been so high.

The training program delivered by Tl'azt'en Nation lasted the longest of the ten First Nations Partnership Programs to date. The program was established to train child care staff for a new child care centre in the community of Tache. The students who enrolled needed academic upgrading, which meant that the typical two-year program had to be extended over three years. Students began the program gradually, combining a reduced course load with ongoing preparatory work in basic academic and study skills and personal life skills. Just when students were ready to assume a full course load, a series of tragic events necessitated several temporary cessations of the program. Each of the ten students enrolled in the program in 1996 experienced the death of one or more relatives during the course of the program. Nonetheless, not only did the partnership program conclude successfully in 1999, it was the first post-secondary program of any kind offered within the community to achieve a high degree of success.

Initially, there was a high turnover rate among the instructors and only one or two recognized Elders in the community to add cultural perspective to the curriculum. By the start of the third year, however, the program had been relocated from the adult learning centre to the local school. This helped the students become more involved in the school itself, especially since their own young children were right down the hall. The students persevered, and by June 1999, eight of the original ten had completed the program. Some are now taking the lead as managers and staff of a child care centre in Tache; others are working in related fields. Three graduates took it upon themselves to submit a successful proposal to the federal government, which enabled the creation of an Aboriginal Head Start program in their community. This program helps parents introduce their preschool children to reading, to their traditional language, and to their First Nations cultural background.

The partnership program's impact on the community was profound, triggering an overall revitalization of Carrier culture and pride. More than a dozen older community members were eventually brought into the program. Through their stories they were able to convey that the Tl'azt'enne people have their own story, a connection to the land, and distinctive cultural traits. This knowledge was empowering for many people in the community who had lost touch with their roots.

In a final class project, the students created cultural activity kits for use in early childhood education. These included moccasins they had made themselves and other traditional crafts and foods. A highlight of this cultural renaissance occurred at the graduation ceremony, when the seldom heard sounds of Carrier chanting and drumming drifted through the town.

Amelia Stark, administrator for the Tl'azt'en Nation, attributes much of the training program's success to the community location: "Because they didn't have to leave [their community] to take their training, the students never forgot that their community needed them to complete the program. And what they learned fit with the community, because they had the community right here to test out their ideas and get feedback."

Treaty 8 Tribal Association Partnership

The partnership with Treaty 8 Tribal Association illustrates the challenges of incorporating cultural content and maintaining students' social connections in their communities when students leave their community to study.

The Tribal Association comprises six culturally and linguistically diverse First Nations: Doig River, Blueberry River, Saulteau, West Moberly, Halfway River, and Prophet River. The association was formed for administrative, financial, and representational purposes; the cooperative delivery of the ECCD program is but one example of the association's accomplishments. Each of the six communities was invited to recruit and finance up to three students.

The fifteen students from these small reserve communities were separated by driving times of two to five hours. Following an intensive preparatory program during which they lived together dormitory-style and became a cohesive group, the students moved to the central location of Fort St. John to undertake the full program. Many brought along their children and spouses. This was the first time most of the students and their children had lived off-reserve. Some students were able to arrange for their children to be cared for by family members in their home communities while they travelled to Fort St. John to spend each school week in the program. One such student from Saulteau First Nation later remarked: "I have no regrets in taking the two-year course, although it kept me away from my husband and children every week. From the program I learned my culture and Elder teachings that will remain forever in my heart."

Because most Elders lived in outlying communities, they were not available often to contribute to the class. Instead, the program mounted several theme weeks when Elders came to Fort St. John for a few days at a time to provide intensive training in specific cultural practices. As well, students undertook cultural projects in their own communities that included interviewing local Elders. The experience of connecting with Elders, which the Elders also enjoyed, was a first for many of the students. At the final graduation ceremony, more than eighty Elders, community resource people, and practicum supervisors from in and around Fort St. John were thanked for their contributions to the program.

As with Tl'azt'en Nation, renewed cultural pride was evident at the ceremony as men from the various communities drummed the students into a large auditorium filled with families and supporters. Drawing on the colours of the medicine wheel used by some First Nations people, the students' gowns were red to symbolize thought and connectedness, their caps were black to symbolize activity, and they carried white flowers to represent maturity and wisdom. Standing under a giant dream catcher symbolically interwoven with Indigenous and Euro-Western cultural threads, fourteen students were honoured for successfully completing the training program. Subsequently, most were employed in their own communities in child care centres, Head Start programs, preschools, and other human service programs.

The partnership with Treaty 8 Tribal Association illustrates the flexibility of the Generative Curriculum Model in adapting to diverse community needs. The solution of centrally locating the training program was a viable way to offer it to geographically separate communities while still incorporating the key elements of the Generative Curriculum Model. However, it was noted during the program evaluation that the highly circumscribed participation of Elders and other community resource people did not yield the same degree of community involvement that occurred in the other partnership programs. In addition, the costs of travel and accommodation for students and Elders drove the overall costs of this program higher than the other partnership programs, despite its shorter duration.

Fostering Greater Understanding of First Nations in the Wider Community

In addition to core courses in child and youth development, early childhood education, and communications, the Generative Curriculum Model includes five practicum experiences. Ideally, the practica would take place in child care centres within the communities where the training programs are located. This has seldom been possible, however, because most of the communities we have partnered with have been in the process of developing child care programs; indeed, the training program has been part of that development. As a result, most practica have taken place in non-Indigenous child care centres in surrounding communities. This has created challenges but has also provided valuable opportunities to strengthen cross-cultural understanding outside the participating communities, extending the transformations made possible by the Generative Curriculum Model.

In each partnership program, the community identifies suitable, accessible practicum sites for students to develop applied competencies. Practicum supervisors at these sites are recruited by First Nations community administrators. The supervisors are important not only because government requires successful practica to qualify for ECE certification but also because students depend on them to provide a safe, non-discriminatory atmosphere in which they can develop new skills. Program graduates often describe the role of the practicum supervisors as pivotal in their ability to cope emotionally and function effectively as trainees. Many of the students recall that their own experiences in formal education settings *eroded* rather than *promoted* positive concepts of themselves as worthy and capable learners. Many remember painful incidents involving racism. Practicum supervisors vary in their receptivity to the distinctive cultural viewpoints and approaches that the First Nations students often bring to the practicum setting. An instructor in the Cowichan Tribes partnership notes:

> You had to be very careful how you matched it up ... Do a lot of interviewing, discussing. It has to be a place where ... it's not going to be really negative. When placing a First Nations student there has to be an openness. You can give them [practicum supervisors] a list of competencies, but they may interpret it in a way that the student doesn't or we don't. So there's a lot of ground work to be done in matching.

In recognition of the central importance of practicum supervisors, the university-based team developed print materials to prepare practicum supervisors to support First Nations students effectively. These materials emphasize that First Nations students benefit from a settling-in period when they first arrive at the practicum site and request the practicum supervisor's encouragement and patience. Some students arrive at the practicum site without ever having been in a non-Indigenous child care setting prior to taking the training program. For some of the students, the practicum placement is their first job. If students have left their own children behind in their home community, they are likely to feel uncomfortable or anxious at first. Given these realities, students appreciate an opportunity to develop some familiarity in the setting before being asked to perform. The print materials suggest that practicum supervisors model how to interact with the children in the centre and how to lead activities.

It has been critically important to raise awareness among prospective practicum supervisors that First Nations students are likely to have styles of interaction different from those that supervisors typically encounter with practicum students from other programs. For example, First Nations individuals often prefer to interact one-on-one with children rather than in groups. They tend to be soft-spoken, warm, and open toward children while not being highly directive or appearing outwardly enthusiastic. Above all, practicum supervisors need to be aware that First Nations students bring special strengths and talents to their work as child care practitioners.

Ultimately, the training practica contribute significantly to increased awareness in the wider ECE community about what First Nations practitioners bring to the field. Non-Indigenous practicum supervisors frequently remark on the quiet manner that many students display with the children in their centres:

> They needed time to feel comfortable, but once they settled in, we found that the students developed good rapport with the children. Very personal and warm. And because they had already been learning from Elders in the Generative Curriculum program, they offered us good ideas about how to involve the Elders who come to our centre, which was a real contribution since this has been a challenging area for us ... We learned so much from having the three students doing their practicum in our centre. They have a quiet, personal way, which the children found non-threatening, warm, and engaging. We found that although they were very non-directive, they soon gained a certain authority with the children that had a very calming effect on the whole centre, including many of the staff. (Practicum supervisor, Tl'azt'en Nation)

The practica have built bridges among neighbouring Indigenous and non-Indigenous communities, fostering an atmosphere of greater understanding and trust between people involved in providing child care services in the same region. This has resulted in collaborations for sharing knowledge and resources. In one instance, program graduates in a First Nations community regularly provide guidance about the needs of Indigenous children in a largely non-Indigenous centre, and they visit that centre to lead activities that enhance all children's appreciation of First Nations cultures and languages. In exchange, a child care specialist from the non-Indigenous centre provides help to the newly established child care centres on the reserve. Some program graduates now serve on regional ECE boards, and many have become part of the professional ECE organization in their province. At a recent annual convention of the Early Childhood Educators of British Columbia, seventeen program graduates were in attendance, five gave presentations, and several broached First Nations issues in open forums.

Features and Challenges of Community-Based Post-Secondary Education

The Generative Curriculum Model is more than a training program that happens to be located within a community. The model places community needs and interests before institutional preferences, giving rise to greater flexibility and variability both in program planning and delivery and in the post-program phase.

The child and youth care diploma program was designed to take place over two years; however, the program implementation phase has ranged from nineteen to forty-two months across the first ten partnerships. Variability has depended on the expressed needs of the community partner. In the Treaty 8 Tribal Association partnership, the shortest program to date, students were in class longer each day and took fewer, shorter breaks between terms. This approach to program implementation was motivated by the uncertainly of continued funding and the fact that students had moved away from their villages – and in some cases their families – to a nearby town and were eager to return home. The partnership with Tl'azt'en Nation, as discussed earlier in this chapter, has been the longest program to date, in response to students' needs for preparatory work and several temporary cessations of the program when tragic events occurred in students' lives.

A factor that sometimes affects the pace of program delivery is the difficulty that some students' husbands have with their wives being occupied outside the home and with the prospect of their becoming more confident, independent, and employed. An effective response to this reaction has been to welcome family members into the classroom, which ultimately improves program support among students, their families, and the community as a whole. An instructor with the Cowichan Tribes partnership notes:

> In our program ... there was a lot of suspicion about what was going on, by family members. Like, why were the moms spending so much time away from home? Just because [those family members] didn't know what was happening. That's something we tried to address by bringing family in or just

making contact with the family ... They often wanted to come see where their mom or their partner spent the day. And that seemed to really help and it also seemed to help them see there was a need for support. (Instructor, Cowichan Tribes)

Finally, because many of the students' families depend on seasonal hunting, fishing, and berry picking for subsistence, the program accommodates time off for students to pursue these important activities. These examples all illustrate the practical consequences of placing community needs ahead of typical institutional requirements.

A First Nations Partnership Program does not end on the day that delivery of all the courses is completed. To support students in successfully completing all of the program requirements for the diploma, the partnership continues actively throughout a post-program phase ranging from six to twelve months. In the partnerships to date, an average of 70 percent of the students have had small but necessary steps to complete, usually a final round of supervised practicum training or final assignments for one or two courses. The most prevalent challenge to completion of the full diploma program is the required university-level English course, which communities access through local colleges or through Open University distance education. While students often need to improve their proficiency in writing, reading, and speaking, many struggle with the content and teaching model of the available English courses. Students and program administrators have recommended development of a new English course that is sensitive to Indigenous students' needs, encompasses positive First Nations literature, is tailored to the communication task demands of practitioners in early childhood and youth services, and is taught on-site.

The average cost per student in the first ten partnership programs has ranged from $4,000 to $5,000 per term, which is slightly higher than the cost per student in other post-secondary ECE programs. However, higher completion rates indicate that in terms of community investments, the First Nations Partnership Programs are significantly more cost-effective than other programs. Cost-effectiveness improves when there are more students in a cohort. Other factors, especially transportation requirements and the availability of community resource people to serve in instructor roles, cause considerable variation in costs as well. The two programs with the highest costs to date have been those that were most remote. In the Treaty 8 Tribal Association partnership in northern British Columbia, students from six disparate villages moved to a central location. This strategy reduced the costs and hazards of daily travel during dangerous winter weather, but it increased the cost of rental accommodation and transportation of Elders from villages to the centralized classroom. The living allowance component of program funding was higher than for any other program, approximating the support costs for students who move away from home to attend universities and colleges. In the Tl'azt'en Nation partnership, students moved on three occasions to the closest urban centre for periods of up to two weeks to access suitable practicum sites. More remote program locations are also more costly for institution-based partners to visit.

Despite the slightly increased costs associated with delivering the Generative Curriculum Model, at least 80 percent of the program expenditures in each partnership to date have remained within the community. Communities deliver the program in their own facilities, provide their own administrative and support services, and contract with instructors who are either community members or have been recruited to the community for the duration of the program. The communities raise all of the funds for both community-based program implementation and institution-based program support. While this contributes to the community's sense of agency and control in the partnership – and its pride in successful implementation – it also places a significant financial burden on some. The most serious challenge for the partnerships has been the absence of a base of operational funds, independent of funds raised by the community, to support the involvement of the university-based team. The institution-based team requires funding to develop new course materials, update existing curriculum, travel to and liaise with communities, and participate in community-initiated fundraising activities.

The overall costs of mounting a partnership program are higher than the tuition fee cost of program delivery through a university or community college system. Direct comparisons are inappropriate, however, since tuition fees do not cover the full costs of program development and delivery, as is the case with the First Nations Partnership Programs. Throughout the programs' seventeen-year history, we have tried without success to secure base-budget support from the university system. Nonetheless, if one compares the post-secondary tuition fee schedule to the full per-student cost of the First Nations Partnership Programs – calculated on a student completion basis – the cost of the First Nations Partnership Programs is significantly lower, given the much higher completion rates.

A challenge for both the institution-based team and the partner communities has been a lack of funding to support involvement during the critical pre-program period (see Chapter 2) and during post-program follow-up. Funding for education and training is typically tied to the specific period when courses are being delivered. Also, funding is often based on a narrow conception of what is involved in education and training. Thus, several of the community partners have had difficulty obtaining sufficient external funds to support Elders' involvement, the intergenerational facilitator's role, students' travel to and from practica, and community events to elicit broad social participation in the program. For the institutional partners, inadequate funding has seriously curtailed the capacity to reach out to prospective community partners, travel to communities, build relationships in communities, support community efforts to mobilize resources, and help create the conditions that enable program delivery.

An important part of delivering community-based ECE training programs involves student access to placement sites for practica, and this has proven challenging. Flexibility in determining what constitutes a valid practicum experience needs to be communicated across the profession and to the provincial licensing authority. Without such flexibility, First Nations students who live in remote communities are significantly disadvantaged in accessing ECE training. In addition, child care centres in the closest large community can experience incredible pressure from the demands for practicum placements that come from various programs in outlying communities. Creating practical training opportunities by involving community children in short-term activities is one way some programs have tried to fill the gap in existing available placements. Innovative ways of providing practicum-type activities have been found:

> They have one classroom and they bring the kids in from the community and they have one licensed person in there and it's called "preschool practice" and they get their experience that way. (Practicum course instructor, Tl'azt'en Nation)

> When I was teaching a class [and realized,] "Okay, we're not going to be going to a licensed facility before the next class," so they would do things with their kids at home ... the kids up at the school ... So they tried out some of the assignments at least with whatever kids were available and then we had to get them all together for the licensed facility practicum ... Maybe if that was built in to a program, saying that it's okay to do that. (Practicum course instructor, Onion Lake First Nation)

One of the greatest challenges that arises from basing a university-accredited program in communities is that the activity is invisible to the on-campus teaching, learning, and administrative community in the partnering institution. This separation limits the potential of the Generative Curriculum Model to effect change within mainstream post-secondary education. A large proportion of the total number of First Nations students enrolled at the University of Victoria has been students participating in the ECCD training program. Because they are outside the walls of mainstream classrooms, however, their absence has been more salient than their presence as members of the university community.

Reflections on Community-Based Education

Through its community-involving process, the Generative Curriculum Model has the potential to reveal and bring into focus elements of the social ecology of the First Nations community. How community members construe those elements and their perceptions of the implications for child care and development have been the subject of extensive dialogue and debate in the ten partnership programs to date. These elements have included the roles of parents, siblings, other children, and grandparents and other Elders; historical experiences with school; literacy; culturally influenced learning styles; culturally appropriate instructional processes; traditional language; approaches to problem solving; the impact of social relationships on cognitive performance; Indigenous definitions of intelligence; cultural goals of maturity and their influence on guided participation; communication with children; interaction between children and adults; and children's social partners. Cultural activities led by the Elders during the training program often include traditional ceremonies and practices and the collection of items and documents of cultural importance.

The Generative Curriculum Model's community-based delivery methods have particular relevance for post-secondary training in marginalized communities in Canada and around the world. However, we believe this model of program delivery has the potential to transform a range of post-secondary education and training programs that are delivered in institutions, removed from the interests and needs of communities. The Western philosophical tradition and, by extension, mainstream educational programs, tend to frame universal questions of who we are and where our society is going in abstract terms, devoid of any reference to, or experience of, particular times and places. This method has resulted in diverse schools of thought, but it is debatable whether it has improved our lives, particularly in relation to the human services, which necessarily revolve around people in particular times and places. By truly grounding learning in the heart of communities, we may be able to foster the transformation of human services that has been called for now for several decades.

Transforming Knowledge through Trust and Respect

If it's done the way it's always been done, none of our First Nations members are going to get educated. First Nations people have always been so laughed at, so put down, and have dropped out of school so often that when they do want to continue their education, they can't even get in – and if they do, they'll give up too fast because it's not culturally relevant.

– Saulteau social development officer,
Treaty 8 Tribal Association

Cultural Safety in Education

Imagine that to pursue professional training, you are required to live and study every day in a culture whose values, traditions, language, and cultural practices differ significantly from your own, and where your own culture is devalued and misunderstood. In this context, you are expected to master academic material that most of your fellow students find challenging even though it is grounded in their own culture. Unlike them, however, you have little or no access to the support of friends, family, teachers, and community members whose life experiences are similar to your own. Your prospects of finding work after graduation in a community of your peers are limited. Compounding these difficulties, any supportive programs available for you on campus or in the community are perceived by many to be an unnecessary drain on their taxes, as crutches you could do without if only you were a competent, mature, and resourceful person like them.

That such a scenario strikes us as overblown and parodic illustrates how far removed we are from having experienced anything of the sort. Until we have experienced being the Other in a culturally alienating environment, most of us are blind to the finely woven support systems that provide us with the safety we need to learn and explore. We take such supports as much for granted as the air we breathe; indeed, we can hardly distinguish them from that air, so natural are they to us. We reside in the realm of cultural safety. It is precisely because that realm is so familiar to us that the concept of cultural safety may strike us as exotic when it is named – especially when it is named by someone who has primarily experienced its absence.

The First Nations Partnership Programs were not designed with the notion of cultural safety specifically in mind. Indeed, the term did not exist in the qualitative research literature until 1992, when it was introduced as part of a controversial nursing and midwifery educational initiative in New Zealand (Dyck and Kearns 1995). The cultural safety debate in New Zealand is situated in a political landscape and an historical context of cultural oppression and growing resistance by Indigenous people to their subordinate social and economic position within society. In Canada, Aboriginal populations are engaged in similar struggles to reclaim the legitimacy of their cultural beliefs and practices and to heal the deep wounds caused by assimilationist policies and years of officially sanctioned racist attitudes and practices (Royal Commission on Aboriginal Peoples 1996).

The standards for cultural safety defined by the Nursing Council of New Zealand (quoted by Papps and Ramsden 1996) are intended to encourage nursing students to reflect on their cultural identity and the impact of their culture on their professional practice. Rooted in deep concern for the deterioration in the health of the Maori people after 150 years of European influence, the concept of cultural safety originated at bicultural meetings that were widely supported by nurse educators and Maori student nurses. Within their training programs, nursing students examine their beliefs, values, and assumptions about others, seeking to become regardful of cultural differences in the broadest sense.

Against the backdrop of the cultural safety debate in New Zealand, Isabel Dyck and Robin Kearns (1995) examined the conceptual challenges of culturally safe research practice. Their conclusions are similar to those reached by us and by our First Nations partners in the evolution of the Generative Curriculum Model: "Cultural safety requires that the taken-for-granted character of health care interactions be unveiled and that their power-ladenness be exposed. There is, therefore, a profoundly ethical content to cultural safety" (ibid., 142).

The concept of cultural safety did not explicitly enter the dialogue that led to the First Nations Partnership Programs; however, it was implicit in the words of Meadow Lake Tribal Council Executive Director Ray Ahenakew, who envisioned community-based training as the environment in which "the richness of knowledge in our communities could be fully considered in a new kind of program."

Cultural safety might be defined as feeling safe to express one's perspective and behave in accordance with one's own culture – acknowledging, accepting, and affirming cultural identity, history, values, beliefs, styles, and practices. Cultural safety is essential for effective learning, and it is precisely what is absent in mainstream educational settings for many minority students. The result of its absence is low participation and completion rates. Many First Nations students experience isolation and stress when placed in culturally alienating learning environments. A study of educational outcomes at the University of British Columbia's Native Education Centre found that First Nations students were often afraid to continue their studies, citing experiences with racism and resultant feelings of shame and inferiority (Mirehouse 1994). The presence of a student cultural cohort was a motivating factor for many of the students in choosing to attend the University of British Columbia's centre, along with their expectation that its programs would respect their First Nations heritage and include personally relevant perspectives. The students recognized that to engage in skills acquisition and growth, they needed to experience a degree of comfort and be free of the significant distractions of cultural alienation and racism. In other words, they needed to experience cultural safety in education.

Cultural safety in the First Nations Partnership Programs has proven to be neither an extension of mainstream best practices in ECCD nor an intended outcome. Rather, it has been an emergent quality of learning processes and practices that are wholly embedded in the cultural lives of minority students. In this respect, our experience has been distinct from that of the nursing and midwifery education initiative in New Zealand. Cultural safety has enabled students in the First Nations Partnership Programs to develop the skills they need to critically analyze the contributions of Euro-Western theory and research, allowing them to choose with confidence what best fits their cultural community.

Four Key Factors

In the First Nations Partnership Programs, four interrelated factors are seen to engender cultural safety: community-based delivery, the Generative Curriculum Model, the reflexive orientation of instructors, and the student cultural cohort (see Table 7). These factors do not simply involve adding cultural sensitivity or specific cultural examples to pre-existing courses, nor can they be understood in isolation from one another. Each factor is essential. Working in concert, they create the enabling conditions for experiencing cultural safety within a community of learners. These conditions avoid replicating the obstacles cultural minority students typically encounter and yield an atmosphere of trust and respect.

Community-Based Delivery

In education, as elsewhere in society, difference is often viewed as deficiency, engendering negative judgments and pressure to conform to the discourse, values, and practices of the dominant culture. The transition from majority to minority status that occurs when First Nations students are obliged to leave their communities to pursue university studies is often traumatic for them. This is noted by the student advisor for an innovative Northern Student Education Initiative created to support Indigenous students in making a successful transition to urban life in the Edmonton area:

> When students are not successful in completing the academic year, it is seldom academic work which has defeated them. Instead, it is often the barriers and events outside of school which have interfered with student success. Students face a diverse set of pressures, stresses and expectations from themselves, family and friends. Life away at school can be a lonely and frustrating experience. (German 1997, 37)

Community-based delivery of education does not by itself ensure cultural safety. However, making it possible for minority students to complete university-accredited programs without leaving their cultural communities is the place to start. Those who have been involved in delivering the First Nations Partnership Programs are unequivocal in identifying community-based education as a prerequisite for academic success:

> Living on reserve for practically their lifetime, then moving to a whole different environment, a lot of students face ... cultural shock if they go to an urban centre for their schooling ... A majority of my students have families, and for them to attend university they try as much as they can to take their family, to not separate their family unit. The students' children have a lot of problems living in the urban environment because it's a whole different environment, which is stressful on the student and the children. (Administrator, Onion Lake First Nation)

TABLE 7

Cultural safety in education

Cultural safety	Process	Outcomes
Community-based delivery	• Community involvement in all stages, including curriculum co-construction • Community support for learners • Community guidance for instructors (e.g., on cultural knowledge, community history, and goals for children)	• Supports for students • Social cohesion • Community revitalization
Generative Curriculum Model	• Integrating cultural traditions, practices, and values into curriculum • Involving Elders and community resource people	• Generated curriculum • Relevance of coursework • Interest in learning • Support in learning/ growth from Elders • Restoration of cultural beliefs, values, and practices as foundation of community-based programs
Reflexive instructor orientation	• Reciprocal teaching and learning • Respect for knowledge "all ways"	• Learning "all ways": institutions, communities, individuals • Unlearning of expert-presumption of universal validity of knowledge and expertise • Student and instructor equality
Student cultural cohort	• Peer support • Team building • Constructing meanings and methods through dialogue	• Increased social support • Social cohesion with community • Networking across participating communities • Psychosocial healing • Enhanced completion rates

Our experience shows that locating education and training in students' own communities, where they retain the social and practical support afforded by their circle of extended families and friends, not only keeps students motivated but also contributes to their gradual emergence as leaders in the community-wide dialogue on child care:

> I got support from community members. I think it helped me a lot. It really brought up my self-esteem, my concept of self. It gave me a goal of knowing that these people, I guess, in a way, look up to me. So, I needed to finish and succeed in this child and youth care program for the betterment of myself and my community. (Student, Cowichan Tribes)

> I didn't feel alone. I felt like there was someone standing there with me. Whenever there was a problem, I could go to my family and talk to them about things that had happened in the program and we'd talk it over. (Student, Cowichan Tribes)

> I think a lot of things have changed because of the students ... [The child care centre is] something that we never thought would happen because Lytton was dying, you know. There was nothing here really. But with people like the students, they make things come alive, do something for the community in the community with the people. (Elder, Nzen'man' Child and Family Services)

For obvious reasons, place is paramount in delivering culturally desirable education. In their own communities, students are surrounded by daily reminders of their cultural heritage, thus the obstacle of being the Other is removed. And because the education program has ready access to the knowledge that resides within the community, learning is grounded in the traditions and contemporary values of the students' cultural community.

Creating conditions of cultural safety for students who are not part of the dominant culture involves an appreciation of place and a willingness to engage in partnership. As a First Nations educator from Saddle Lake, Alberta, notes in her research on the conflicts students from cultural minorities face with identity issues, being forced to relocate into the dominant culture of mainstream post-secondary education creates all of the stresses of "living in a foreign environment" (Steinhauer 1998, 115). Similarly, an Australian study on Aboriginal students' perceptions of school proposed that cultural safety in education necessitates that the learning environment mirror the language, customs, attitudes, beliefs, and practices of the students' cultural community (Maxwell, Hansford, and Bennett 1997). An earlier investigation of culturally relevant education for Native Americans stressed that a "lack of incorporating aspects from students' real lives in the school program denotes an environment of non-support of the worst kind" (Gipp and Fox 1991, 60).

Merely transporting mainstream education and training – no matter how culturally sensitive – into Aboriginal communities does not respect the knowledge held by community members. For this reason, community-based delivery of education is not a stand-alone component of cultural safety but the springboard for bicultural curriculum development.

Generative Curriculum Model
The Generative Curriculum Model is distinguished by its respect for the cultural traditions, beliefs, values, and life experiences of students and instructors, including active participation by Elders and other respected community members. The generative framework for curriculum development encourages students to view various conceptualizations of ECE through the lens of their cultural communities. The beliefs and practices of those communities are reinforced through discussions with Elders and through cultural activities that bring ceremonial traditions and storytelling into the classroom:

> Students began to see their own older relatives as sources of wisdom. (Instructor's assistant, Nzen'man' Child and Family Services)

> The good part was the Aboriginal-based part – learning more about the olden-golden age from the Elders. The Elders were awesome. (Student, Nzen'man' Child and Family Services)

> The Elders told us how they were, growing up, their traditions, how things change over time, like child care. It was good to know how they were brought up and how they were disciplined back then. (Student, Nzen'man' Child and Family Services)

> This program is real life. It's not just theory or book-oriented, it's about what you're really going to be dealing with when you finish. This program is about the community and about the culture. (West Moberly education coordinator, Treaty 8 Tribal Association)

The flexibility and participatory nature of the model that is used to co-construct curriculum yields a high degree of cultural relevance and community specificity. How and what students learn in the classroom has meaning in a community's cultural life, enabling First Nations students to experience education as insiders – a fundamental condition for emergent cultural safety:

> The program has really opened up my eyes; it has given me a chance to express myself in the curriculum itself. (Student, Nzen'man' Child and Family Services)

> The curriculum refers to the medicine wheel, but in Carrier culture they don't use the medicine wheel and the students don't care about it, so sometimes we use the potlatch idea. We replace content that doesn't fit here or doesn't seem relevant with content that does fit – that comes from here – to make it relevant. (Instructor, Tl'azt'en Nation)

> One of the things that was critical to being successful [was] the way that we ... presented the material [–] always keeping that philosophy in mind and respecting that the Indigenous way has a different framework. (Instructor, Nzen'man' Child and Family Services)

When community-based delivery is coupled with the Generative Curriculum Model, students are strongly motivated to apply their learning to their different roles in the community, including those of parents and early childhood educators. Nancy Anderson, a graduate of the Treaty 8 Tribal Association partnership, now works at the Cree-ative Wonders Head Start program on the Saulteau Nation's reserve in Moberly Lake, where she provides a culturally sensitive school readiness program for preschool children. Anderson grew up speaking Cree, the language of the Saulteau people, and she regularly modifies nursery rhymes, plays, and songs into Cree. She credits the First Nations Partnership Program with enriching her knowledge of her culture and with helping her integrate her cultural knowledge and skills into her child care practices:

> There was always something in my heart that drew me to love and help children; it was like a calling ... From the program I learned my culture and Elder teachings that will remain forever in my heart. I firmly believe that reserves need preschool programs to help children get ready for kindergarten, and I really believe that the children in the Cree-ative Wonders program are developing their social, intellectual, spiritual, and physical needs. They are learning their culture and they love it.

Lois Andrews, a graduate of the Lil'wat program, reflects on how the First Nations Partnership Program has influenced her work in the community:

> One of the most important goals of our class should be to learn our basic culture and our language and to apply it in our daycare as much as possible. And then families who don't know any of our basic language, they can learn it too through their children, and then in that way it is touching everybody. Before I felt like I was useless or good-for-nothing. But now it is, hey, I can do anything. I can go further and do what I want. As long as my family is there with me I think I can accomplish anything. It seems that every situation that comes along in my life, it comes out through the classroom. It's like, this is just what I wanted to know.

The emphasis on community relevance in ECE training is widely supported by the literature on cultural relevance as the contextual vehicle for constructing meaning in education. As Bruner puts it, "It is culture that provides the tools for organizing and understanding our worlds in communicable ways" (1996, 3). The evolution of the Generative Curriculum Model demonstrates, as well, that for cultural safety to be an emergent quality of instruction, those who teach must be prepared to accept the challenges posed by reciprocal learning.

Reflexive Instructor Orientation

First Nations partner communities recruit instructors from inside and outside their culture, depending on the availability of community members with an ECE or related background. Most of the training programs have had at least one Indigenous instructor. While a shared student-teacher heritage creates obvious benefits in terms of familiarity with cultural traditions and values, the First Nations Partnership Programs experience underlines the importance of a reflexive orientation for effective teaching, whether by Indigenous or non-Indigenous instructors. In a culturally safe learning environment, instructors and program administrators respect the students' preferred styles of communicating and interacting.

To be effective, instructors need to bring a reflexive orientation to the classroom that involves openness to difference and respect for diverse sources of knowledge, with particular attention to the experiential knowledge of students and Elders. As discussed, collaborative cultural construction requires a high degree of student participation. In turn, the generative and bicultural framework of the First Nations Partnership Programs causes many program instructors to reassess their own teaching styles and to recognize opportunities for personal growth and change.

Professional development has not historically focused on a reflexive orientation that leads teacher trainees to examine how their own experiences and cultural values shape their attitudes and interactions with students from other cultural communities. Teachers are typically trained in a linear and sequential manner of instruction that is characteristic of Western culture but not well suited to engendering cultural safety in education (Stahl 1992). Teachers who work with minority students need to become aware of the ways in which they themselves are embedded in their own cultures.

As a starting point for the First Nations Partnership Programs, we acknowledged that non-Indigenous educators are not positioned to be solely responsible for making valid decisions about how to extend the reach and relevance of ECE training in Indigenous communities. As Taylor (1994) asserts when discussing the orientation that teachers should bring to working with students from cultures other than their own, non-Indigenous teachers of First Nations students must be willing to learn and to experience instances of cultural disequilibrium.

Our experience supports research by Wilson (1994), which found that First Nations students make conscious choices about teachers with whom to engage in learning. They value approachable, available instructors who they see as genuine and caring individuals. Students in the First Nations Partnership Programs have described situations where instructors contributed to an atmosphere of trust and cultural safety by asking "how we feel, how we would handle things, how things fit for us." The students' experiences reflect a conscious decision by instructors to replace expert-driven education with true bicultural partnership methods and processes that engage students and teachers in mutual exploration and problem solving:

> I was going through a lot of hard times, but the teachers, they catch you up on it, and they were aware of the situation – like personal problems. So I find that that's nice. It's like they're your friend as well as they are your teacher. (Student, Lil'wat Nation)

> They showed you visually, hands-on; they gave you ideas. There wasn't a right or wrong way. It was always the right way, just different learning. So that was really nice, that you weren't wrong, because that's really scary. If I'm told I'm wrong, it gives me the initiative to give up. (Student, Nzen'man' Child and Family Services)

The support from instructors was good. It made you feel like you wanted to be there, that you were part of a group, that you mattered. (Student, Nzen'man' Child and Family Services)

The experiences of Linda McDonell and Martina Pierre, instructors with the Cowichan Tribes and Lil'wat Nation partnerships respectively, illustrate the diverse ways that cultural safety may be engendered in educational settings by Indigenous and non-Indigenous instructors alike.

Possessing strong interpersonal and listening skills as a recognized ECE leader in British Columbia, McDonell jumped at the chance to teach in the partnership program with the Cowichan Tribes. Like a number of program instructors, McDonell is not a First Nations person. Throughout the program, she was careful to make links between Elders' teachings and the classroom materials she presented. McDonell felt that her role was to help students create these links on their own, and today she is a stronger advocate than ever for cross-cultural awareness in educational programs:

There is tremendous value in the bicultural aspect of the program. The students came to realize the value of the mainstream perspective and develop a dual kind of perspective that will serve them really well in the field.

What McDonell hadn't anticipated was her own personal growth within the program. Although she was asking students to explore their culture, their roots, and their family connections, she was initially unprepared when they asked her to do the same:

I talked a lot about my grandmother and my parents. I realized how little I had really listened to their words. I hadn't heard them as teachings. The process really strengthened my own understanding of where my values and beliefs come from.

Martina Pierre, a member of the Lil'wat Nation, was seconded from her regular position as the director of the Cultural Centre at Lil'wat to work as part of a team of three instructors. As noted by a student in the program, "the process in the classroom incorporated culture. Martina was always speaking our language and especially when the Elders came, Martina would speak to them in our language because they didn't always understand English." Pierre often used her training in linguistics to help students uncover the beliefs and practices of the Stl'atl'imx people through an analysis of the root meanings of concepts conveyed in the traditional Lil'wat language. For example, in one classroom setting with Elders present, she was teaching a unit on the topic of planned change – how to plan for positive change in a child's life. She asked the students to suggest definitions for the term "planned change," then asked the Elders how these definitions might be expressed in Lil'wat. The suggestions the Elders provided translated into English as "to move," "to join with another," "to listen with empathy," and "to make something happen." These definitions conveyed a sense of planned change specific to their traditional culture, and the actual Lil'wat words carried suggestions on how this change could be brought about. By involving the Elders and the Lil'wat language in her lesson, Pierre found a way to make the idea of planned change come into focus in both a present-day and a traditional cultural context.

Student Cultural Cohort

The group identity that forms when students share a common past and a common sense of belonging engenders what Sparks (1998) calls "a community of assistance." Students in the First Nations Partnership Programs provide a great deal of support to each other. For example, the seventeen students who entered the partnership program at Onion Lake, Saskatchewan, in 1996 formed such a tight bond that they soon referred to each other as sisters. One of the students notes:

> We had a lot of support for one another ... Whenever we tried to give up, we kicked each other. We kept telling each other, "You can't [quit]. It's not long. It's the last year." That's how things were. There were [so] many things going on in our lives that we tried to give up, but we didn't. We just kept each other going.

At the graduation ceremonies in 1998, the entire community celebrated the fact that all seventeen students would graduate that day and receive their diploma in child and youth care. Because the students were eager to continue their education, the University of Victoria agreed to mount a pilot program whereby eight of them would work together to pursue their bachelor's degrees in child and youth care. This meant that they could undertake a full undergraduate degree program without leaving Onion Lake, marking a significant step in the evolution of the First Nations Partnership Programs.

The concept of a student cultural cohort was brought into the realm of cultural safety in education by historical tensions between the Cree and

Dene communities represented by our first partner, Meadow Lake Tribal Council. Tribal Council administrators recognized that diverse linguistic strengths and preferences and cultural traditions among the Cree and Dene students in the cohort called for the creation of a learning environment where students would feel their own culture and language were respected and where they felt comfortable to participate without fear or censure. The administrators called on the skills of a senior community member, Louis Opikokew, who had personal relationships with Elders in each of the nine Cree and Dene communities. Every week, Opikokew arranged for an Elder from one of the communities to travel to the classroom, rotating visiting Elders so that all of the communities and their distinctive cultures and dialects were represented. Each week, Opikokew would review the questions for Elders suggested in the course materials, select and revise them, and translate them into Cree or Dene. Ensuring representation of each student's cultural heritage and community in the teaching and learning process contributed to the atmosphere of cultural safety.

Respect and cultural relevance were identified in the Meadow Lake program as two of the pieces necessary to fit together the enabling components of cultural safety. Later, some students in the British Columbia Cowichan Tribes program who came from nearby First Nations communities but had different cultural traditions recalled that they were initially disappointed that their cultural knowledge and practices were not explicitly reflected by Cowichan Elders in the generative curriculum. This disappointment gave way to an emerging sense of shared First Nations identity:

> Because we had a number of students from different tribes on Vancouver Island, there was this frustration in the beginning that "this isn't my community you're talking about" ... and suddenly, I think the relevance across communities came through. There was a shared sense of the importance of traditional teachings and the differences across the communities. (Instructor, Cowichan Tribes)

Students in the Cowichan Tribes partnership experienced education as grounded in First Nations culture – not because they saw themselves as a homogeneous or even a dominant cultural group but because differences were acknowledged and respected. This respectful acknowledgment is diametrically opposed to the denigration or invisibility minority students typically experience in post-secondary education. This may seem obvious at first glance. It is important to recognize, however, that a student cultural cohort should not be a taken-for-granted component of culturally safe education for minority students. Rather, it should be a constant reminder of the need for refined analysis of how to generate curriculum in an atmosphere of trust, where debate and differences yield academic achievement.

Reflections on Cultural Safety

Over the course of ten First Nations Partnership Programs, cultural safety in education has emerged as the pivotal concept in our efforts and those of our Indigenous partners to create a learning environment that redresses the long-standing failure of mainstream post-secondary education to value the culture of minority students. We have come to see that the catalyst for enhanced individual and community capacity to provide culturally desirable child care services is very often students' new-found awareness of their cultural heritage.

The benefits of cultural safety in education enrich both the learning process and its outcomes, leading to increased personal and community capacity. Students in the First Nations Partnership Programs acquire what a Tl'azt'en Nation administrator describes as "a sense of involvement, a sense of ownership in their education." Being engaged in post-secondary education that validates their culture and their life experiences makes learning relevant to individuals and their communities. An Indigenous instructor in the partnership program with Nzen'man' Child and Family Services, Dr. Lisa Sterling, commented on how a culturally safe environment is conducive to expression and consolidation of Indigenous knowledge:

> This program didn't "give" students their Indigenous voice. They already had that. What it gave them was an opportunity to use that voice and, as a group of Indigenous people, to hear each other and to learn together. To evaluate Western ideas and explore Indigenous values and what those could mean for child care practice. And then to decide and create for themselves how to bring their Indigenous viewpoint into models that combined many viewpoints on how to promote children's development and cultural identity. It was a safe environment and the students felt encouraged to express who they were and the Indigenous knowledge they had.

In the First Nations Partnership Programs, cultural safety requires a transfer of power from educator to learner. By embracing effective learning as an "all ways" integrated process that is inseparable from the learner's cultural community, community-based education for minority students can transform knowledge itself, replacing the power of exclusionary curriculum content with the power of discovery. Students who experience cultural safety in education can ask themselves, "What of us is in here?" and answer by pointing to the rich diversity of values, traditions, and practices that situate their lives inside their cultural community.

Asserting the Power of Not Knowing

I said to my soul, be still and wait without hope,
For hope would be hope for the wrong thing; wait without love,
For love would be love for the wrong thing ...
Wait without thought, for you are not ready for thought.
So the darkness shall be the light, and the stillness the dancing.
            – T.S. Eliot, *East Coker*

Evaluating Program Outcomes

Within the tradition of strategic planning that currently dominates program planning and delivery in both public and private sectors, positive program outcomes are the logical consequence of a process of rigorous planning in which a program's mission, goals and objectives, timelines, and outcome indicators are formulated at the outset and monitored at every stage of program implementation to ensure that initiatives stay on track. Program successes that occur in the absence of this linear model of control are seen as happy accidents that cannot be replicated in other settings, thus leaving no practical or theoretical legacy. Our experience with the First Nations Partnership Programs challenges this orthodoxy. In partnership with communities, we have developed and tested a principle-driven process for program planning and delivery that is designed to encourage the emergence of the unique and unknown. This model has proven successful in each of the ten groups of communities where it has been tested. The First Nations Partnership Programs have exceeded our expectations, generating benefits for program participants, their families, and their communities.

From 1998 to 2000, we undertook a comprehensive evaluation of the first seven partnership programs. The evaluation showed that in all seven partnerships, the Generative Curriculum Model led to unprecedented educational and vocational outcomes and to personal and community transformations that reached far beyond the classroom. We coined the term "generative capacity building" to capture program participants' experience of the training program as a process that led to reverberating ripple effects in their lives and the lives of their communities. The partnerships were found to have created new interpersonal relationships, new ways of relating between cultural communities and mainstream institutions, new ways of teaching and learning, new knowledge, and new or syncretic models for supporting children and families. None of these outcomes would have been possible within a mainstream, expert-driven program planning and delivery framework.

Across all seven programs, graduates viewed their success in terms not only of their academic achievements but of their emerging roles as community advocates and respected resources for their family members and friends. Community administrators reported that the First Nations Partnership Programs supported self-determination in their communities and renewed capacity at the community level to provide quality child care and development programs that embody First Nations cultural traditions, values, and practices. Community mobilization to improve conditions for children and families was identified as an important dimension of program effectiveness.

Five antecedent conditions were identified as enabling the teaching and learning processes that led to successful outcomes:

- *partnership*, especially the reciprocal guided participation of willing community and institutional partners
- *community-based delivery* that enabled community inclusion in all phases of program planning, delivery, and refinement
- *student cohort involvement* in their own professional development
- *open architecture* of curriculum that required community input
- facilitation of *cultural input* in curriculum

Participant accounts suggested that the combined effects of these conditions accounted for the partnerships' success. Together, these conditions enabled the cultural fit and social inclusiveness of the training process and curriculum content. In turn, the training program resulted in outcomes that were consistent with community goals.

Individual Goals

In the first seven partnerships, 102 of the 118 students (86.4 percent) who enrolled in the child care training program completed one year of full-time university-accredited study (see Table 8 for more educational and vocational outcomes). For students in British Columbia, this resulted in eligibility for basic certification in ECE by the provincial Ministry of Health. Students completing the full two years (77.3 percent) were eligible for a university diploma as well.

A recurrent theme in the program evaluation was the congruence that graduates experienced in a training program that focused on their cultural and geographic community – its goals for children and families, socio-economic circumstances, readiness, and strategies for responding to the needs of children and youth. Many students contrasted this congruence with previous experiences in mainstream educational institutions, which they described variously as "totally white," "impractical," "culturally con-tradictory," "spiritually bankrupt," and "foreign." Because the Generative Curriculum Model's both/and approach presents Euro-Western theories and research alongside the traditions, values, and practices of the students' own culture, the curriculum resonated with the realities of their daily lives.

Positive psychosocial development among students, including those who did not complete the two-year program, was one way participants gauged program effectiveness. For example, eleven graduates reported sharing new knowledge and skills about child development and their First Nations

TABLE 8

Educational and vocational outcomes

86.4% of students completed one year of full-time, university-accredited study

77.3% of initial enrolees completed a full two years, to achieve a diploma in child and youth care (compared with a national completion rate of 40% and below among First Nations students in other post-secondary programs at the time of data collection)

95% of graduates (students completing one or more years) remained in their home communities

65% of graduates introduced new programs for children, youth, and families

13% of graduates joined the staff of existing services

11% of graduates continued on the education and career ladder, working toward a university degree culture with their adult children who were now raising children of their own. Over 80 percent of graduates reported that their parenting and grandparenting skills and their confidence had improved significantly. This program impact has particular importance for the partnering First Nations. To illustrate the point, consider that the communities involved in the four most recent partnerships have a total population of 5,100. A total of 53 students in the participating communities are parents or grandparents to 186 children. Clearly, enhanced transmission of knowledge, skills, and enthusiasm about child development and parenting represents a substantial impact on the future of the community as a whole.

Significant psychosocial healing was reported by 92 percent of the students across the seven programs (see Table 9 for dimensions of positive change spontaneously mentioned by program participants). Evaluation interviews revealed the extent to which many students had previously internalized negative stereotypes of themselves and their cultural heritage, as well as the extent to which they experienced the First Nations Partnership Programs as a healing journey for themselves and their communities. Many students described feeling more positive about their potential to take control of their own lives and to make valued contributions in their families and communities.

Working through trauma experienced in residential schools was another recurrent theme in the interviews. Many graduates talked about having missed the foundational experiences of being parented effectively because they, or their parents, had been forced to attend residential schools far from their families and communities. Many of the graduates reported that

TABLE 9

Dimensions of positive change

Indicator	Percentage
Enhanced self-confidence	93.2
Better communication skills	92.0
Feeling respected by others	88.9
Effective advising of others on child rearing	88.7
More effective as a parent	87.0
More clarity on cultural identity	87.0
Better family life	86.7
Healthier lifestyle	75.5
More connection with community	71.0
More participation in cultural activities	68.0

painful memories had emerged when they took part in class discussions, listened to the stories of the Elders, and completed assignments reflecting on their experiences of childhood and parenting. Participants linked the availability of social support within the student cohort, within a culturally safe classroom environment created by the instructors and Elders, and within their own community as an important factor that enabled them to use their memories of childhood traumas constructively in their program of professional development.

Community Goals

Certificates and diplomas were neither the only nor the ultimate criteria that evaluation participants used to measure program effectiveness. Most important was the fact that 95 percent of program graduates remained in their communities, thereby strengthening community capacity to provide culturally appropriate services for children and families. As many evaluation participants noted, few if any benefits accrue to the community when students go away to university and do not return – or when they come back, in the words of an Elder, "as strangers with alien ideas."

Two communities offered financial data to compare the benefits of the First Nations Partnership Programs to other avenues for post-secondary education and training. Both of these communities reported providing at least $17,000 per single student per year when community members moved away to attend university or college. If students moved their children and partners with them, the communities' expenses were higher. They reported that no more than 30 percent of community members who had gone away for education had completed their training. Of those who had, many have not returned to the community. Thus, the return on their investment in terms of capacity built to achieve community development goals was far superior in the First Nations Partnership Programs compared with the conventional practice of supporting First Nations students to go away for post-secondary training.

The evaluation research showed that the First Nations Partnership Programs had effectively supported community-identified goals for expanded service delivery. As a group, community-based administrators across the seven partnerships prioritized three objectives: to provide safe, developmentally supportive care for children; to enable parents to pursue education and employment; and to ensure the reproduction and reconstruction of Indigenous culture through programs for children and families. Within one year of program completion, graduates had initiated many types of programs for children, including out-of-home, centre-based daycares; in-home family daycares; Aboriginal Head Start; infant development programs; home-school liaison programs; parent support programs; individualized supported child care for children with special needs; language enhancement programs; youth services; school-based teacher assistance/learning support; after-school care programs; and a children's program in a women's safe home.

Pivotal Concepts

During the two-year period of the training program, the Generative Curriculum provided graduates with opportunities to consult with their communities about how children were understood within a particular First Nations frame and how best to support optimal child development through programs and services. Three key themes were evident in reports by graduates and community members on what had emerged for them over the course of the training program as pivotal concepts around which program development should revolve.

Holism

Child development is viewed holistically in the partnering First Nations, with the many aspects of a child's body, mind, and spirit, as well as his or her past and future, seen as intertwined and requiring recognition, nurturance, guidance, and respect. This view permeates community decisions about what child care and development programs should entail – for example, a proactive, developmental approach to the "whole child" that includes nutrition, preventive health, socialization, education, and Indigenous language and culture. This approach is consistent with a national call for integrated and intersectoral coordination (Romanow 2002).

Social Inclusion

One Elder who was interviewed during the evaluation explained that concepts that distinguish children according to age, stage, or abilities are not particularly meaningful or wanted in her community:

> The idea of early childhood and ideas like disabled children, or that some children have special needs and some children are gifted – these ideas don't come from us. They are not Aboriginal ideas. They come from white people, and from cities. All children have gifts and are gifts from the Creator. We don't like to box people up and separate them out. We've seen how that can be used as a way of getting rid of people, of boxing them up and shipping them out, out of the community to special schools or what have you. Until

we were forced to send our children away to school, we always kept all our children with us, and all together, in families, and we want that again.

Many other participants echoed the holistic, inclusive lifespan perspective and the spiritual convictions evident in this Elder's words, also referring to "all the children" "all together" and expressing a desire to create a welcoming centre in the community that people would experience as a kind of home and family.

Community-Involving Services

The goal of improved conditions for children's health and development was seen by community leaders and students as dependent upon the goal of supporting family wellness. Thus it was conceived that child care and development programs should reach out to secure the active involvement of parents, grandparents, aunts, uncles, and others who care for children. As a child care practitioner in one of the communities said:

> Parents in our community either went to residential school or were raised by parents who did. Many never had a chance to experience childhood themselves. They are just beginning to heal, and just beginning to learn how to be parents.

A goal of the child care and development strategies in these communities has been to provide a respectful, safe, socially supportive centre for parents and guardians to access not only child care but also, equally importantly, information about healthy lifestyles, parent education and support programs, residential school recovery and healing programs, community events, and service referrals as needed.

The examples below illustrate the initiative of program participants in strengthening services for children and families in their communities in ways that were consistent with local developmental goals for children and grounded in the cultural values and understandings of the students' communities.

In the five Cree and four Dene communities represented by Meadow Lake Tribal Council, graduates started daycares and other child and family services at their home reserves in remote parts of northern Saskatchewan. Some took up leadership roles in health and social development planning within the Tribal Council offices. One graduate joined the staff of a safe home for women, where she introduced play, education, and emotional support programs for the women's children.

The partnership with the Cowichan Tribes occurred in a semi-urban environment and was the only program in which classes were held on a college campus located on federal reserve land. Graduates applied their training in a variety of sites, including child care and parent support programs, probation services, and college student services. Of the original twenty-two students, eight continued to complete their third and fourth years of university study toward a degree in education or human services.

In the Onion Lake First Nation program, half of the seventeen graduates in the community of seventeen hundred were hired as staff at child care programs in their villages or as assistants at the community school. One graduate started a daycare in the main community at Onion Lake. Ten program graduates continued with First Nations Partnership Programs in a pilot project that enabled them to take third- and fourth-year courses in child and youth care while remaining in their community. Six of these students graduated with a bachelor's degree. Combining distance learning and face-to-face meetings in classrooms on the reserve using the Generative Curriculum Model, these individuals have forged a new path for students in other partner communities who may wish to ladder to the next rung in their career development.

Graduates of the Nzen'man' Child and Family Services partnership are involved in a variety of centre-based and in-home child care programs and after-school care. In the sparsely populated rural area of the Fraser Canyon where this partnership is located, graduates are also serving First Nations children and families through mobile outreach programs.

A range of new daycare and other child- and family-centred programs were started and staffed by graduates from the six villages that make up the Treaty 8 Tribal Association. Included among the programs is the Cree-ative Wonders child care centre at Saulteau reserve, which emphasizes Cree language and cultural learning in the early years. Continuing the bicultural approach that underlies the training program, some graduates are involved in English literacy programs that help parents prepare their children for school.

A question of central interest in the evaluation was how the strong cultural component of the training experience had influenced the programs that graduates have created. Observations in centre-based care programs in the communities provided many examples of cultural components, including:

- children's books created in their traditional language about families in the community

- the colours and teachings of the medicine wheel incorporated into the lessons
- masks and legends incorporated into the classroom
- labels on classroom items in the traditional language and in English
- child-sized drums and group drumming songs
- traditional crafts, such as the making of button blankets, miniature tee-pees, moccasins, basketry and bead work, and including the use of traditional tools and materials
- model clan houses decorated with symbolic animals in the playground
- an emphasis on nature in storytelling, lessons, and artwork
- infusion of First Nations spirituality in stories, art, and ways of describing people and events
- cradle boards for infants
- traditional foods such as bannock, smoked fish, and dried meat
- organization of children into traditional clans for small group activities
- creation and use of the traditional talking stick for structuring talking circle time
- healing circle talk to provide support in response to distressing events
- "time in" rather than "time out" in response to children's challenging behaviours
- preparing for traditional community events, such as powwows
- learning traditional sustenance activities such as gathering mushrooms and berries for food and reeds for baskets; preparing fish, fruits, meats, and leather; following the seasons and the rhythms of the community.

The evaluation revealed distinctive characteristics in the ways that program graduates approached caregiving, both in practicum situations and in their work after graduation. For example, graduates created programs that were flexible in response to seasonal variations, unanticipated opportunities, and the needs of individual children, parents, or caregivers. Such flexibility is not often found in mainstream child care settings. Program graduates tended to adopt a non-authoritarian, child-centred approach to directing children's behaviour in program activities. Consistent with the latter, they tended to accept a wide range of individual differences among both children and their parents and showed a reluctance to label children (e.g., as having special needs or disabilities). Echoing their experiences in the child care training program, graduates also tended to involve Elders and parents in meaningful ways in the programs they joined or created.

The success of program graduates often served as a catalyst for community healing. This theme was eloquently expressed by Grand Chief Edward

John of the Tl'azt'en Nation in a keynote address at a conference of the British Columbia Aboriginal Child Care Society. Grand Chief John recounted the ceremony that was held in June 1999 in his home village of Tache to honour the eight students who completed their coursework in the child care training program:

> Our Nation has been faced with many tragedies, and sometimes we have wondered how we can ever survive all the struggles that have come to us. And it was just this June that we suffered the loss of one of the old people in our community through an act of violence. And this event seemed like yet another blow to the Tl'azt'enne people, and many people were wondering how we can ever survive all the tragedies and overcome our problems and begin to grow stronger. But then we were so fortunate to have the ceremony and celebration to recognize the completion of coursework in child and youth care by eight women of our community. The way these women persisted, continued, and persevered for the years they took these university classes – what they did is an honour to us, the Tl'azt'enne people. And they are the hope for our future, because they will become the leaders in our community and they will show others that education is the tool for surviving our tragedies, beginning to heal, and growing stronger. They are the members of our community who will guide us in supporting our children – our future.

A Template for Social Change

Two constructs emerged from the evaluation – and from our years of experience with the First Nations Partnership Programs – as critical for describing and explaining the programs' processes and outcomes: social cohesion and social inclusion. Together, these processes provide a template for social change.

Social cohesion encompasses the many facets of community involvement in administering the training programs, the participation of students in cohorts, and the bringing together of multiple generations to support the development of the community's children and families. When participants described the community transformations that had resulted from the program, they highlighted an enhanced willingness and capacity of individuals to participate in ways that built trust and reciprocity, met their shared needs, mobilized new knowledge and resources in programs of action, built on organizational strengths, and increased community stability. Social cohesion is offered here as a critical wraparound concept that represents: (a) a characteristic of the community partners that enabled them to enter effectively into partnership with the university; (b) a characteristic of the process of community involvement in program delivery; and (c) a dimension of community life that was enhanced as a result of program delivery.

The concept of social inclusion captures the links that were strengthened between individuals and groups outside the community. The impact of the First Nations Partnership Programs on social inclusion was vividly illustrated when several graduates took active roles in two province-wide conferences, one on early childhood education and one on Aboriginal child care. The graduates spoke out on issues of funding for child care and training, and presented a range of ideas for responding to cultural diversity in child care programs. As an outcome, social inclusion refers to the recognition and participation of community members and university partners in each other's venues and in the society at large. Creating professional networks and building on mutual learning relationships were seen as important components of capacity building.

Representatives of the four partnering post-secondary institutions identified varying effects of program participation on institutional structures and practices. For example, the Saskatchewan Indian Institute of Technologies (SIIT) had a long-standing relationship with Meadow Lake Tribal Council. The institute was involved in the delivery of the first year of the ECCD program after the initial demonstration partnership program concluded. As well, SIIT participated in the subsequent three-way partnership with Onion Lake First Nation. As a direct result of its involvement in the First Nations Partnership Programs, SIIT gained a new program offering as well as a new approach to serving its First Nations constituencies (SIIT has conducted four of its own two-way partnerships with other tribal councils in Saskatchewan). Collaboration between SIIT and the First Nations Partnership Programs team at the University of Victoria continues through the sharing of new and updated course materials and program outreach strategies.

As a direct result of the First Nations Partnership Programs, Malaspina University-College gained a new program offering in Child and Youth Care, which it has adapted to the unique circumstances of the college's location on Cowichan Tribes reserve lands. The program is offered on campus on an ongoing basis, and students can enrol without being part of a community cohort. Malaspina has developed several additional community-based initiatives. Individual students and Elders participate regularly in class meetings. As well, the First Nations Partnership Programs team at the University of Victoria has entered into agreements with the college to work with other First Nations communities in the region. In the evaluation, college administrators attributed the experience of partnership program delivery using the Generative Curriculum Model to new understandings among their faculty and administrators about how to incorporate culture in coursework and how to involve Elders in course design and delivery. As a result of the partnership program, the college instituted a full-time staff position, that of Elder-in-residence, for a senior member of the Cowichan Tribes. The first Elder to fill this role was Louise Underwood, who had been the intergenerational facilitator for the First Nations Partnership Program with the Cowichan Tribes. During the evaluation, Underwood commented:

> This program was the very first time we had Elder teachings going into Malaspina [University-College] classrooms. And now we have about two hundred resource people from Cowichan and various other First Nations. We have developed an open dialogue with the community – the doors are open both ways. And we have the child and youth care program, resulting from the first partnership. So there is a real community feel about that program, with Elders and resource people coming and going, and students going out to the community, which after all is the way it should be – a huge circle of learning and teaching and support.

The First Nations Partnership Programs, and especially the Generative Curriculum Model that evolved from them, broke new ground for the University of Victoria. Although community-based programs were not new to the university, the co-construction of curriculum by community members and a university-based team was a new approach. The university has gained credibility with many First Nations as an approachable and responsive institution as a result of supporting an unprecedented number of First Nations students in completing a program of studies that led to Ministry of Health certification, a university diploma, increased First Nations labour force participation, and increased capacity for community-operated services. During the evaluation, Valerie Kuehne, former associate vice-president (academic) of the University of Victoria, noted:

> These partnerships have been very exciting for us. They have not always been easy, but always worth the investment of time and energies that have gone into them. The partnerships have demonstrated a new kind of outreach from the university to communities, especially remote communities, and they have been very effective. Do I think there are challenges that remain? Absolutely. There is the matter of making the successes of these partnerships more visible, and therefore more likely to be supported and expanded. There are funding

issues and questions of the applicability of this type of partnership program, and this type of curriculum model, to other fields of professional training. Overall, though, I think the School of Child and Youth Care and the university have benefited tremendously from the opportunities to partner with First Nations in this way.

Reflections on Program Outcomes

We opened this chapter on program outcomes with a poem that evokes the powerful potential of indeterminacy. In contrast to a model of rigorous planning in which a program's mission, goals and objectives, timelines, and outcome indicators are rigidly formulated at the outset and monitored at every stage of program implementation, the Generative Curriculum Model that evolved through the First Nations Partnership Programs asserts the power of not knowing program outcomes in advance.

No one could have anticipated in the initial stage of each of the partnership projects exactly what the co-constructed curriculum would include. Few practitioner training models invite students, much less communities, to engage in a process of co-construction. Yet, when we reflect on the evolution of the Generative Curriculum Model, it is clear that its success derives from our acceptance of not knowing – not knowing where exactly the partners' work would lead, not knowing which aspects of mainstream theory and research would fit and which would need to be reconstructed by community participants, not knowing what would constitute "quality care," and not being poised with vats of knowledge to pour into the empty vessels of ECCD trainees' minds.

In contrast to the colonialist presumption of knowing what is best for Indigenous people, the Generative Curriculum Model assumes that First Nations communities themselves are in the best position to define their communities' goals for their children and families. Much potential exists for mainstream post-secondary institutions to work in genuine partnership with First Nations to improve outcomes for Indigenous students, their families, and their communities. Significantly, the approach employed in the First Nations Partnership Programs runs counter to the approach often used in working with communities with a history of disempowerment. The First Nations Partnership Programs' guiding principles build on community strengths, provide for community involvement at every stage of program planning and delivery, and support the emergence of new knowledge rather than imposing Western-based theory and practice that may not be relevant to First Nations unless it is placed in dialogue with Indigenous knowledge.

In mainstream education at all levels, positive outcomes are generally limited to individual educational and vocational goals. In contrast, a wealth of individual and community benefits has flowed from the First Nations Partnership Programs. The principles of the partnerships offer an alternative to mainstream post-secondary education and development assistance training that can be adapted to other education programs and capacity-building initiatives in health, social services, and other fields. It is our hope that the model's potential to transform individuals and communities may be realized in a wide variety of settings.

Supporting Children and Families with Sustained Community Transformations

8

> [We wanted to] establish our own daycare, operated by our own people, carrying on our own traditions and values. We have done that. Parents are happy when their children go to this child care program. They develop good habits, have good nutrition, early learning, especially cultural learning, and socialization. We have support from the chief and council and administration here, and the staff who graduated from the post-secondary program with [the University of Victoria] are very happy to be working in our own community. The different departments here work together – the Health, Child Care, Education and Training, Wellness, Economic Development, Social Development – we all work together, and that contributes to the success of our programs.
>
> – Christine Leo, former director of Community
> Advancement Programs, Lil'wat Nation

Sustaining Capacity

What has been the return on community investment in delivering a community-based post-secondary program deeply informed by Indigenous knowledge and goals for children's development? This was the question asked by three of our First Nations partners four years after thirty-five members of their communities had graduated from the ECCD program. At the suggestion of community advancement administrators at Treaty 8 Tribal Association, Tl'azt'en Nation, and Lil'wat Nation, a follow-up sustainability study was conducted from 2002 to 2004 (Ball 2004). The study found sustained community transformations building on capacity developed during the First Nations Partnership Programs (Ball 2005).

Through interviews, questionnaires, and forums, seventy-six people from the three groups of communities participated in the research. In addition, the programs that graduates had innovated were profiled through a review of program manuals, policies, and service utilization records, as well as through direct observations of how the programs were reaching out to children and families. The research also explored the ways in which the communities had achieved program implementation, including challenges, benefits, and next steps.

The study found that thirty-three of the thirty-five graduates were working, most in career-relevant practice in their communities. Graduates were building community-based infrastructure to support the holistic development of young children and their families. The study showed that the First Nations Partnership Program's emphasis on Indigenous knowledge, the focus on understanding child and family development in students' communities, and the creation of a cohort of professional early childhood practitioners had prepared graduates to develop and operate programs suited to local needs and goals of families and children.

The communities' involvement with the First Nations Partnership Programs began with their commitment to rebuilding their capacity to support children in the context of the family and the community. The design and delivery of new programs in these First Nations illustrate the benefits of long-term, comprehensive visioning and planning, good community governance, and a steadfast commitment to the youngest generation's well-being as a priority for community development. Christine Leo, then director of Community Advancement Programs for Lil'wat Nation, expressed her community's belief that its future rests on the health and wellness of its children:

> Lil'wat Nation strongly believes in Aboriginal title and rights and our sovereignty over our lands. We need to provide support for families and specifically for young children, and ... for families that are having trouble caring for their young children ... Another value is that we want our children to have cultural training. A few years ago, we did a labour analysis and needs survey, and our first priority was post-secondary training in early childhood, so that we could establish our own daycare, operated by our own people, carrying on our own traditions and values.

The communities have realized the benefits and learned what it takes to move beyond the rhetoric of "culturally appropriate" and "community-driven" services to engage incrementally in steps that lead to the goal of comprehensive, culturally grounded, community-based supports for children and families.

A point made repeatedly by Aboriginal leaders in Canada as they work to strengthen their communities' capacity to mount and operate services – or to take over staff positions in existing services – is that Aboriginal people want to learn from the mistakes of others. They have no wish to replicate the fragmentation, inefficiency, and philosophically dissonant concepts that often drive mainstream health and social services and community development in Canada. In the words of a representative of one of British Columbia's inter-tribal health authorities:

> Yes, we need training. But what do we want to train our people to do and to become? The transition to Aboriginal control should not mean simply Aboriginal people taking over white jobs, doing things in white ways. We want to do things in Aboriginal ways. We need training that will support our members in remembering their cultures and creating Aboriginal services that are really Aboriginal.

The kind of training a community makes available to its members affects both the graduates' and the community's readiness to create services that respond constructively to the goals of families for their children rather than to discrete problems (e.g., a speech-language difficulty) or needs defined in terms of specific services (e.g., child care). In contrast, mainstream training and services are overwhelmingly problem-driven and conceptualized outside the context of the family and the community. Throughout the two-year post-secondary program, members of the participating communities discussed what child and family wellness means within the historical context, culture, and lifestyles of their people. Across all the communities, the pivotal concepts of holism, social inclusion, and community-centred development elaborated in Chapter 7 were returned to again and again. Training that is community-based, community-driven, and community-involving, and that builds on community-specific cultural knowledge and practices, helps ensure that graduates can deliver the services and supports the community needs in ways it will accept and appreciate.

Community Approaches

The approach of all of the communities involved in the First Nations Partnership Programs has been to increase access to services in a number of ways, and not just through geographic proximity or by providing financial subsidies but also by ensuring cultural safety and by providing services that meet locally determined needs and goals. The communities have embarked on long-range plans that move away from fragmented, individual-focused service delivery toward community-centred models that integrate health and development programs. Clear operational links are being created between child care and other health, social, and cultural programs intended to benefit children and families.

Treaty 8 Tribal Association

By the time the students graduated, three of the six First Nations in Treaty 8 Tribal Association had developed new facilities and services for children. Because of other pressing priorities, one community had been unable to develop services, but two others had used existing educational facilities to mount new child care programs. Two Aboriginal Head Start programs – both staffed by program graduates – are now located in two of the smaller communities, Blueberry River and Saulteau First Nation.

The remote communities of Treaty 8 Tribal Association face special challenges because of their small population base. Funding is often allocated on a per capita basis, which limits the communities' ability to realize a broad range of integrated, community-appropriate services. Diane Bigfoot, the Tribal Association's education coordinator, spoke of the ongoing effort to strengthen ECCD capacity:

> The training in early childhood care and development brought forth more programs – not only child care – but for children and families, and it brought these to the communities. This is still growing. Two of the First Nations just started a child care and development program – expanded beyond the Aboriginal Head Start program. They are sharing, and this sharing is also an outcome of the communication and understanding that developed between people who were originally students in the post-secondary training together. It is good to see the communities working together in this way.

Although some variability exists among the small communities that form the Tribal Association, the emergence of a community-based service approach was evident in each village. The six First Nations each have a school, a child care centre, and a health care centre in or near their largest on-reserve population centre. The health care centre typically consists of three or four small offices where similar services are effectively clustered together. Because of the small number of community members and visiting specialists involved, the services delivered through these offices are coordinated.

Communication, service memory, and intersection occur because, in general, everyone knows everyone else. ECCD programs and specialist services remain essentially fragmented, however, with regard to sources of funding, service mandate, scope of practice, and accountability requirements. According to Diane Bigfoot, the presence of trained community members keeps attention focused on the importance of culturally appropriate programs for children and youth: "There are all sorts of programs running – even if the administration changes or the political level is turbulent, the services continue. This is very important."

Tl'azt'en Nation

Before the training program began, Tl'azt'en Nation received Aboriginal Head Start and other funding that enabled them to construct a licensed child care facility in an unused wing of the school in Tache, the largest on-reserve population centre. During the training program, students planned the Nation's first child care centre, which they named *Sum Yaz*, or Little Star. They developed operational policies and procedures, created curriculum activities to teach young children their traditional Carrier language and promote a positive Tl'azt'enne identity, and negotiated contracts with a carpentry training program on reserve to create furniture and toys for the facility. Students completed their final practicum at the new centre. Eight of ten students who completed the training program were hired as staff in the child care and Aboriginal Head Start programs.

Both of the children's programs have received excellent evaluations from the regional ECE licensing officer and from Aboriginal Head Start. Children come by bus from the villages of Binche and Dzitl'ainli, twenty to forty-five minutes away, to attend the school, Head Start, and the child care program. During the follow-up study, ECCD practitioners, community administrators, and contract service providers described how the child care and Head Start facilities are used as sites for the integration of services. This integration enables access between specialists and children and parents, development of service memory among staff, multidisciplinary professional development for on-reserve staff, and cultural learning for visiting specialists.

The community decided to locate health services, adult counselling, and drug and alcohol treatment services in an area of the village away from the school, the child care centre, and the Head Start facility. Administrators and ECCD practitioners explained that this decision was taken to prevent the spread of illness and to provide some children-only space away from the concerns of adults involved in social services, treatment, and recovery programs.

Lil'wat Nation

Lil'wat Nation has the largest population base among the communities that participated in the follow-up study. About one thousand people live in one main community, and eight hundred others live in four affiliated communities. Together they have established a well-developed planning structure, stable leadership, and a long history of successful development initiatives. In the mid-1990s, Lil'wat Nation decided to plan for comprehensive, integrated child care and development programs incorporating cultural values, heritage language, and cultural literacy. Its goals were to enable parents to take up healing programs, continued education, and employment, and to support the development and cultural identity of young children. As illustrated in Figure 4, their concept for services to families is community-centred, beginning with culturally consistent, quality child care delivered by trained community members in a licensed setting.

In May 1999, just as fourteen of the fifteen students enrolled in the training program were graduating, the community opened a multiplex called *Pqusnalhcw*, or Eagles Nest. The facility, located two hundred metres from a band-operated K-12 school, is a culturally vibrant gathering place that also serves to promote health and wellness for the whole community. Trained community members staff the facility, which functions as a site for the integrated delivery of a range of health and development services.

A large preschool program called *Skwalx*, or Baby Eagle, and an infant care centre called *Tsepalin*, or Baby Basket, are housed in the multiplex, along with an after-school care program that shares some staff, activities, outdoor play space, and equipment with the child care programs. Over time, the services delivered inside the child care centre have evolved to include occupational therapy; special needs child care; developmental monitoring, assessment, and referral; speech-language pathology screening and monitoring; and preventive dentistry. In 2003, the child care programs served 110 children ranging from infancy to six years of age. The community recently added a "language nest" preschool between the multiplex and the school, where graduates of the training program team with Elder speakers of the Lil'wat language to deliver a heritage language immersion program for a dozen preschoolers (McIvor 2004).

The health service wing of the multiplex has a staff room, examination rooms, and a health information and promotion area. Health services offered include drug and alcohol counselling, tobacco reduction, and diabetes

FIGURE 4

Community-based service model with child care centre as integration site

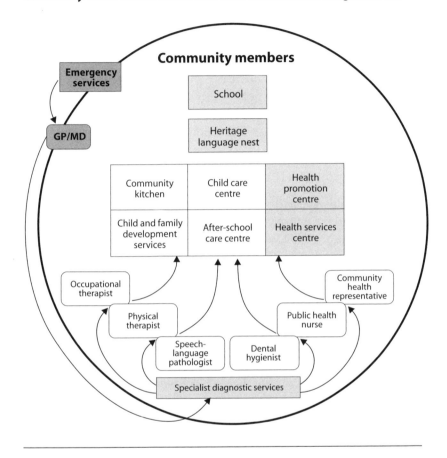

prevention. Also located in the multiplex are a community kitchen and multipurpose rooms that offer a range of family services, as shown in Figure 4.

According to Christine Leo, Lil'wat Nation's former director of Community Advancement Programs: "Capacity increased in our community not only because all but one of the students finished the whole program but also because parents will be able to take advantage of employment and training opportunities now that there is a good daycare right here. And the Generative Curriculum Model meant that our values and language are integrated into the daycare program, so that the children's capacity to use our language and know our culture will be stronger."

ECCD as "Hook" and "Hub"

The First Nations partners that participated in the follow-up study have taken significant steps to support the well-being of children and families. Although each community is approaching service development differently, all of the administrators and practitioners expressed satisfaction with their progress. They are incrementally rolling out services that ensure their communities' children receive quality care. The services are introduced in a way that effectively "hooks" parents, other caregivers, Elders, and community administrators to participate in both child care and in other laddered health and development services built around the "hub" of a child care program (Ball 2005).

Hooks

When community leaders held forums to discuss making ECCD a focal point of community capacity building and infrastructural development, the value of assuring quality care for babies and preschoolers mobilized positive community action. Child care is the central hook that attracts families to new community services and secures their attachment to programs supporting the well-being of all family members. Many of the child care staff interviewed for the follow-up study said that while parents are often willing to seek playmates for their children, respite from the constant demands of parenting, or reliable daycare so they can work, they may be less willing to seek supports or services for themselves or other family members. Parents described how they began by bringing their children for care and then expanded their involvement to access other, co-located services for children. Over time, as they became comfortable with the staff and the quality of care, they came to the centre for social support and services for themselves.

Other hooks for securing family attachment to comprehensive community-based supports for achieving wellness include involving community members in the ECCD training program as guest speakers, mentors, planners, and helpers; co-locating programs with cultural meeting places and community kitchens; and holding events such as open houses and family days that welcome the whole community. In several of the partnering First Nations, child care programs are located with the pregnancy outreach program Best Babies, mom-and-tot groups such as parent-child Mother Goose, language facilitation programs, nutrition workshops, hands-on displays on healthy living (e.g., diabetes prevention, exercise, medication), and similar programs to promote child and family well-being. When parents bring their child for care, they pick up information about other available programs. They see other community members attending these programs. Staff in the centre get to know them and may draw their attention to particular program offerings. Gradually, parents become more involved. They might volunteer to help in the community kitchen or spend time with children in the child care program. After a period of familiarization, they develop a sense of safety and trust in the staff. They may then enrol in a program themselves. As one community member said:

> Ever since this place happened, I feel like people can come out more and get the help and support they need. This child care program has been like a magnet that has drawn us to get together and keeps us here, doing things to help and heal ourselves and that will hopefully make our community stronger and a better place for our children and everyone who lives here and even those who want to move back here.

Hubs

While the hook approach is a child-centred model of service delivery, the hub model centres on families and communities. Services are specifically designed to meet community needs for developmental, social, cultural, and primary health programs, as well as to support children at risk and those with special needs. By setting up their child care centre as the hub of a larger system of community programs and meeting spaces, some First Nations communities have created a service delivery model that is multi-dimensional, accessible, and culturally appropriate.

In the follow-up study, many community members spoke about the concept of early childhood as a foreign idea that artificially segregates young children from "all children" or "the whole community." One Elder said, "Our children need to be understood as part of a whole that includes their family, community, culture, and the natural environment." In these communities, the child care facilities are primary sites for bringing people of all ages together for cultural events and for services and programs that address the well-being of the "whole child" and the "whole family." These include information and education, social support, health, and speech-language services. A grandmother who regularly brings her grandsons to the child development programs explained:

> Our child care is a holistic model, and feels natural to us as Aboriginal people, where we have always seen children and the community as one. Children are the future of our community – they are, or they should be, the centre of everything we do.

Promising Practices

The communities that participated in the follow-up study are addressing a range of needs and goals for children by providing a corresponding range of direct, accessible services and by rebuilding cultural, social, and physical environments for child and family development within a culturally congruent, community-based development model. These promising practices show how holistic thinking, good governance, community-driven training, forethought, and ingenuity can create cost- and resource-efficient service systems that are tailored to a community's culture, circumstances, readiness, needs, and goals.

Each of the partnering communities is different, and the research found variations in how each is able to support the "whole child" within the context of their family and community. Larger communities have more funding, more trained community members, and often a larger group of core leaders in governance and community development, thus they are able to implement more comprehensive training and service programs. Communities with smaller populations – especially those that are geographically remote – have access to less funding, especially when funding levels are determined on a per capita basis. These communities find it difficult to access training, attract and retain practitioners, and provide mentoring and professional development for program staff. Small communities are often less ready to articulate their goals for community development, and they may not have the leadership or resources to advocate effectively for training and service development or to implement long-range plans for community-based services. The follow-up study found that the small communities in Treaty 8 Tribal Association are finding success through working with neighbouring communities to coordinate programs and services. Supporting children and families in small, remote communities across Canada, as Romanow (2002) points out, is a challenge that calls for national dialogue and changes in policies and funding priorities.

First Nations in Canada are diverse; it is unlikely that any one vision, plan, or model will be appropriate for all. As Romanow (2002) and the National Aboriginal Health Organization (2002) emphasize, training programs and service delivery models must be adapted to the realities of different Indigenous communities. Community members need to be directly involved in defining the training and services they need and determining how to organize and deliver them most effectively. Respecting that there are many paths to achieving the goal of community-centred services, most Indigenous communities in Canada advocate holistic approaches to child and family well-being that require partnerships between communities and training institutions, among communities and across sectors. It is clear that capacity-building initiatives must be anchored deeply within each community's socio-historical context, geography, culture, values, and goals.

For those First Nations that are blazing new trails for Indigenous communities across Canada to realize their vision of a comprehensive, culturally fitting, community-centred strategy to address children's development holistically and contextually, the road has been far from smooth. During both the program evaluation and the follow-up study, First Nations and institutional partners described many sources of frustration and challenge: finding and sustaining funding, staying the course over long periods to ensure that programs take root, and encountering duplications in accountability requirements across funders and sectors. They also identified the challenge of having ground-breaking pilot projects recognized and supported in remote rural settings, far from centralized monitoring bodies and campus-based administrators. Institutions must engage in supportive long-term partnerships with communities that will enable the communities to evolve and implement creative approaches over time. Despite the challenges, the communities and post-secondary institutions involved in the First Nations Partnership Programs have demonstrated strong leadership, political will, creativity, cooperation, and persistence, which have resulted in learning and strengthened capacity in communities and universities.

Demographic trends in Canada suggest that the number of young Indigenous children will grow at twice the rate of non-Indigenous children over the next decade (Statistics Canada 2003). A significant funding commitment will be required to support community-driven initiatives for nation rebuilding through community-based post-secondary education in ECCD.

The First Nations Partnership Programs – and the research findings that illuminate the conditions that enable their success – underscore the need for funding agencies, branches of government, regulatory bodies, community administrators, and training institutions to open up the foundations of how education and training, community development, and service delivery are conceived and supported. Each community that shares the goal of developing a coordinated, culturally informed approach to promoting the well-being of children and families must be given enough flexibility and long-term support to evolve and implement its own long-term vision.

Communities that are ready and that have the will to see a vision of rebuilding support for children and families through to successful implementation will need funding and technical support to develop both the hard infrastructure (buildings and equipment) and the soft infrastructure (enabling policies, training in human services, effective governance for service developments and delivery, the appointment of administrators and management) that are required to support that vision. Researchers, too, will need funding to develop community-relevant criteria and tools for measuring program performance and to enable the effective communication of new knowledge so that further promising practices can be identified and shared.

Reflections on Strengthening Indigenous Early Childhood Program Capacity

This book has described an approach that involves First Nations in collaborative partnerships with post-secondary institutions to create and deliver an adaptable ECCD training program. In this approach, community and institutional partners collaborate to generate a curriculum that embodies the community's cultural traditions, values, and goals for children and families while also introducing students to a representative sampling of research, theory, and practices in the Euro-Western tradition. The First Nations Partnership Programs effectively move away from the conventional idea of professional training as the development of an elite class of experts with an elevated claim to knowing what is best for children and families (Dahlberg, Moss, and Pence 1999). Instead, the partnership programs' decolonizing approach recognizes communities' need and desire to develop local capacity to innovate their own programs, guided by their cultural goals and by community-centred models for supporting children and families (Ball and Pence 2002; Ball et al. 2002).

The stories told in this volume convey what has been learned by breaking away from campus-based, mainstream training models and exploring community-centred, co-constructive ways of combining the strengths of cultural communities and post-secondary institutions. Our hope is that this learning will be used to inform other initiatives intended to stimulate social inclusion and cultural revitalization while rebuilding community capacity to support children and families. Sustaining cultural knowledge and ensuring healthy social ecologies where children can thrive requires intercultural partnerships based on trust, reciprocity, and a commitment to long-term engagements. The First Nations Partnership Programs demonstrate the potential that exists for institutional and community transformation when partners anchor development initiatives deeply within the context of local people and exercise the will to act on the principle that communities really matter.

References

Allman, P., C. Cavanagh, C.L. Hang, S. Haddad, and P. Mayo, eds. 1998. A tribute to Paulo Freire. *Convergence* 31 (1, 2).

Armstrong, J. 2000. A holistic education, teachings from the dance house: We cannot afford to lose one Native child. In *Indigenous educational models for contemporary practice: In our mother's voice,* ed. Maenette Kape'ahiokalani Padeken Ah Nee-Benham with Joanne Cooper, 35-43. Mahwah, NJ: Lawrence Erlbaum.

Armstrong, R., J. Kennedy, and P.R. Oberle. 1990. *University education and economic well-being: Indian achievement and prospects.* Ottawa: Indian and Northern Affairs Canada.

Assembly of First Nations. 1989. *Report of the national inquiry into First Nations child care.* Summerstown, ON: Assembly of First Nations National Indian Brotherhood.

Ball, J. 1994. Strategies for promoting active learning in large classes. *Journal of Teaching Practice* 2: 3-11.

–. 1998. Identity formation in Confucian-heritage societies. In *Multiculturalism as a fourth force,* ed. P. Pedersen, 147-65. Philadelphia: Taylor and Francis, Bruner/Mazel.

–. 2000. *First Nations Partnership Programs: Generative Curriculum Model. Program evaluation report.* http://www.fnpp.org/peval.htm (17 August 2005).

–. 2004. *Early childhood care and development programs as hook and hub: Promising practices in First Nations communities.* http://www.ecdip.org/reports/index.htm (18 August 2005).

–. 2005. Early childhood care and development programs as hook and hub for inter-sectoral service delivery in First Nations communities. *Journal of Aboriginal Health* 2 (1): 36-53.

Ball, J., and A.R. Pence. 1999. Beyond developmentally appropriate practice: Developing community and culturally appropriate practice. *Young Children,* March: 46-50.

–. 2000. Involving communities in constructions of culturally appropriate ECE curriculum. *Australian Journal of Early Childhood Education* 25 (1): 21-25.

–. 2002. The Generative Curriculum Model. In *UNESCO-MOST bes practices in Indigenous Knowledge.* Paris: UNESCO.

Ball, J., M. Pierre, A.R. Pence, and V. Kuehne. 2002. Rediscovering First Nations values in child care in Canada. In *Intergenerational program strategies from a global perspective*, ed. M. Kaplan, N. Henkin, and A. Kusano, 83-100. Lanham, MD: University Press of America.

Barman, J. 1996. Aboriginal education at the crossroads: The legacy of residential schools and the way ahead. In *Visions of the heart: Canadian Aboriginal issues*, ed. D.A. Long and O.P. Dickason, 271-303. Toronto: Harcourt Brace.

Battiste, M., ed. 2000. *Reclaiming Indigenous voice and vision.* Vancouver: UBC Press.

Battiste, M., and J. Barman, eds. 1995. *First Nations education in Canada: The circle unfolds.* Vancouver: UBC Press.

Becker, J., and M. Varelas. 1995. Assisting construction: The role of the teacher in assisting the learner's construction of preexisting cultural knowledge. In *Constructivism in education*, ed. L. Steffe and J. Gale, 433-46. Hillsdale, NJ: Lawrence Erlbaum.

Benhabib, S. 1992. *Situating the self: Gender, community and postmodernism in contemporary ethics.* New York: Routledge.

Bernhard, J. 1995. The changing field of child development: Cultural diversity and the professional training of early childhood educators. *Canadian Journal of Education* 20 (4): 415-36.

Bernhard, J., J. Gonzalez-Mena, H.N.-L. Chang, M. O'Loughlin, C. Eggers-Piérola, G. Roberts Fiati, and P. Corson. 1998. Recognizing the centrality of cultural diversity and racial equity: Beginning a discussion and critical reflection on "developmentally appropriate practice." *Canadian Journal of Research in Early Childhood Education* 7 (1): 81-90.

Bernstein, R.J. 1983. *Beyond objectivism and relativism.* Philadelphia: University of Pennsylvania Press.

Bloch, M., and T. Popkewitz. 2000. Constructing the parent, teacher, and child: Discourses of development. In *The politics of early childhood education*, ed. L.D. Soto, 5-32. New York: P. Lang.

Bowman, B.T. 1994. The challenge of diversity. *Phi Delta Kappan* 76 (3): 218-24.

Bronfenbrenner, U. 1979. *The ecology of human development: Experiments by nature and design.* Cambridge, MA: Cambridge University Press.

Brookfield, S.D. 1991. *Developing critical thinkers: Challenging adults to explore alternative ways of thinking and acting.* San Francisco: Jossey-Bass.

Brookfield, S.D., and S. Preskill. 1999. *Discussion as a way of teaching: Tools and techniques for democratic classrooms.* San Francisco: Jossey-Bass.

Bruner, J. 1996. *The culture of education.* Cambridge, MA: Harvard University Press.

Burman, E. 1994. *Deconstructing developmental psychology.* London: Routledge.

Cajete, G., ed. 1999. *A people's ecology.* Santa Fe, NM: Clear Light Publishers.

Chang, H., A. Muckelroy, D. Pulido-Tobiassen, and C. Dowell. 2000. Redefining childcare and early education in a diverse society: Dialogue and reflection. In *The politics of early childhood education*, ed. L.D. Soto, 143-64. New York: P. Lang.

Cochran, M. 1988. Parental empowerment in family matters: Lessons learned from a research program. In *Parent education as early childhood intervention: Emerging directions in theory, research, and practice*, ed. D. Powell, 25-30. Norwood, NJ: Ablex.

Cole, M. 1996. *Cultural psychology: A once and future discipline.* Cambridge, MA: Harvard University Press.

Cook, P. 1993. Curriculum evaluation for the MLTC/SCYC career ladder project: A summative ecocultural analysis. Unpublished report. Meadow Lake Tribal Council, Meadow Lake, Saskatchewan.

Dahlberg, G., P. Moss, and A.R. Pence. 1999. *Beyond quality in early childhood education and care: Postmodern perspectives.* London: Falmer Press.

Dasen, P.R., and G. Jahoda, eds. 1986. Cross-cultural human development. Special issue. *International Journal of Behavioural Development* 9: 4.

Derman-Sparks, L., and C. Phillips. 1997. *Teaching/learning anti-racism: A developmental approach.* New York: Teachers College Press.

Descartes, R. 1960. *Discourse on method.* Trans. L. Lafleur. New York: MacMillan. (Original work published 1637.)

Dyck, I., and R. Kearns. 1995. Transforming the relations of research: Towards culturally safe geographies of health and healing. *Health and Place* 1 (2): 137-47.

Eliot, T.S. 1944. *Four quartets: East Coker.* London: Faber and Faber.

Ermine, W.J. 1995. Aboriginal epistemology. In *First Nations education in Canada: The circle unfolds,* ed. M. Battiste and J. Barman, 101-12. Vancouver: UBC Press.

Foucault, M. 1970. *The order of things: An archaeology of the human sciences.* New York: Random House.

Fournier, S., and E. Crey. 1997. *Stolen from our embrace: The abduction of First Nations children and the restoration of Aboriginal communities.* Vancouver: Douglas and McIntyre.

Freire, P. 1993. *Pedagogy of the oppressed.* Trans. M. Bergman Ramos. New York: Continuum. (Original work published 1970.)

German, N. 1997. Northern student education initiative. *Native Social Work Journal* 1 (1): 33-41.

Gipp, G.E., and S.J. Fox. 1991. Promoting cultural relevance in American Indian education. *Education Digest* 57 (3): 58-61.

Giroux, H. 1989. *Schooling for democracy: Critical pedagogy in the modern age.* London: Routledge.

–. 1992. *Border crossings: Cultural workers and the politics of education.* New York: Routledge.

Goffin, S. 1996. Child development knowledge and early childhood teacher preparation: Assessing the relationship – A special collection. *Early Childhood Research Quarterly* 11 (2): 117-34.

Gonzalez-Mena, J. 2001. *Multicultural issues in child care.* 3rd ed. Mountain View, CA: Mayfield.

Green, M. 1993. The passions of pluralism: Multiculturalism and the expanding community. *Educational Researcher* 22 (1): 13-18.

Greenwood, M., and T. Fraser. 2005. Ways of knowing and being: Indigenous early childhood care and education. In *Broadening and deepening understandings of quality,* ed. V. Pacini-Ketchabaw and A.R. Pence, 41-58. Ottawa: Canadian Child Care Federation.

Greenwood, M., L. Opikokew, M.R. Opekokew, and M.R. McIntyre. 1994. The Elders speak: Of the past, of children and families. Unpublished report, Meadow Lake Tribal Council, Meadow Lake, Saskatchewan.

Habermas, J. 1983. Modernity: An incomplete project. In *The anti-aesthetic: Essays on postmodern culture,* ed. H. Foster, 3-15. Port Townsend, WA: Bay Press.

Haig-Brown, C. 1988. *Resistance and renewal: Surviving the Indian residential school.* Vancouver: Tillacum Library.

Halldorson, L., and A.R. Pence. 1995. FNPP program guide. Unpublished manuscript, University of Victoria, British Columbia.

Ing, N.R. 2000. Dealing with shame and unresolved trauma: Residential school and its impact on the second and third generation adults. PhD diss., University of British Columbia.

Jones, E. 1994. *Emergent curriculum.* Washington, DC: National Association for the Education of Young Children.

Kagitcibasi, C. 1996. *Family and human development across cultures: A view from the other side.* Mahwah, NJ: Lawrence Erlbaum.

Kelly, C. 1990. Professionalizing child and youth care: An overview. In *Perspectives in professional child and youth care,* ed. J.P. Anglin, C.J. Denholm, R.V. Ferguson, and A.R. Pence, 167-76. New York: Haworth Press.

Kerr, M. 1998. Partnering and international health: A subject for ethical enquiry. Paper presented at Partnerships for Health: A Work in Progress, fifth Canadian Conference on International Health, Ottawa.

Kessler, S., and M. Hauser. 2000. Critical pedagogy and the politics of play. In *The politics of early childhood education,* ed. L.D. Soto, 59-71. New York: P. Lang.

Kessler, S., and B.B. Swadener, eds. 1992. Introduction: Reconceptualizing curriculum. In *Reconceptualizing the early childhood curriculum: Beginning the dialogue,* ed. S. Kessler and B.B. Swadener, xiii-xxviii. New York: Teachers College Press.

Ki-Zerbo, J., C.H. Kane, J. Archibald, E. Lizop, and M. Rahnema. 1997. Education as an instrument of cultural defoliation: A multi-voice report. In *The post-development reader,* ed. M. Rahnema and V. Bawtree, 152-60. London: Zed Books.

Kuhn, T. 1970. *The structure of scientific revolutions.* Chicago: University of Chicago Press.

Lamb, M., K. Sternberg, C. Hwang, and A. Broberg, eds. 1992. *Child care in context.* Hillsdale, NJ: Lawrence Erlbaum.

Lather, P. 1991. *Getting smart: Feminist research and pedagogy with/in the postmodern.* London: Routledge.

Le Roux, W. 1999. *Torn apart: San children as change agents in a process of acculturation.* Botswana: Kuru Development Trust and WIMSA.

Lederman, J. 1999. Trauma and healing in Aboriginal families and communities. *Native Journal of Social Work* 2 (1): 59-90.

Lima, E.S., and M. Gazzetta. 1994. From lay teachers to university students: The path for empowerment through culturally based pedagogical action. *Anthropology and Education Quarterly* 25 (3): 236-49.

Lockhart, A. 1982. The insider-outsider dialectic in Native socio-economic development: A case study in process understanding. *Canadian Journal of Native Studies* 2: 159-62.

Lubeck, S. 1996. Deconstructing "child development knowledge" and "teacher preparation." *Early Childhood Research Quarterly* 11: 147-67.

–. 1998. Is developmentally appropriate practice for everyone? *Childhood Education* 74: 283-92.

Lubeck, S., and J. Post. 2000a. Distributed knowledge: Seeing differences in beliefs and practices as a resource for professional development. In *Rethinking childhood,* ed. L.D. Soto, 33-58. Albany, NY: State University of New York Press.

–. 2000b. Creating a Head Start community of practice. In *The politics of early child-hood education*, ed. L.D. Soto, 33-58. New York: P. Lang.

Lyotard, J.F. 1984. *The postmodern condition: A report on knowledge*. Minneapolis, MN: University of Minneapolis Press.

Marfo, K. 1993. Program evaluation comments. Appendix to Curriculum evaluation for the MLTC/SCYC career ladder project: A summative ecocultural analysis, ed. P. Cook. Unpublished manuscript, Meadow Lake Tribal Council, Meadow Lake, Saskatchewan.

Maxwell, T.W., B. Hansford, and T. Bennett. 1997. Aboriginal students' perceptions of school. *McGill Journal of Education* 32 (2): 99-124.

McIvor, O. 2004. Building the nests: Indigenous language revitalization in Canada through early childhood immersion programs. Master's thesis, School of Child and Youth Care, University of Victoria.

McMillan, A.D. 1995. *Native peoples and cultures of Canada: An anthropological over-view*. 2nd ed. Vancouver: Douglas and McIntyre.

Meadow Lake Tribal Council. 1989. Vision statement. Unpublished report, Meadow Lake Tribal Council, Meadow Lake, Saskatchewan.

Mirehouse, G. 1994. The Native Education Centre: Its impact on cultural identity and educational outcomes. Master's thesis, Faculty of Education, University of British Columbia.

Moss, P., and A.R. Pence, eds. 1994. *Value and quality in early childhood services: New approaches to defining quality*. New York: Teachers College Press.

National Aboriginal Health Organization. 2002. *Dialogue on Aboriginal health: Shar-ing our challenges and our successes*. Report on the Aboriginal forum held in partner-ship with the Commission on the Future of Health Care in Canada, 26 June, Aylmer, Quebec. Ottawa: National Aboriginal Health Organization.

Nsamenang, A.B. 1992. *Human development in cultural context: A Third World perspec-tive*. London: Sage.

–. 2004. *Cultures of human development and education: Challenge to growing up African*. New York: Nova Science Publishers.

Pacini-Ketchabaw, V., and O. McIvor. 2005. Negotiating bilingualism in early child-hood: A study of immigrant families and early childhood practitioners. In *Broaden-ing and deepening understandings of quality*, ed. V. Pacini-Ketchabaw and A.R. Pence, 109-26. Ottawa: Canadian Child Care Federation.

Papps, E., and I. Ramsden. 1996. Cultural safety in nursing: The New Zealand experi-ence. *International Journal for Quality in Health Care* 8 (5): 491-97.

Pence, A.R. 1998. Reconceptualizing ECCD in the majority world: One minority world perspective. *International Journal of Early Childhood* 30 (2): 19-30.

–. 1999a. ECCD: Through the looking glass. Keynote address, Early Childhood World Forum, Honolulu.

–. 1999b. "It takes a village..." and new ways to get there. In *Developmental health and the wealth of nations: Social, biological, and educational dynamics*, ed. D.P. Keating and C. Hertzman, 322-36. New York: Guilford Press.

–. 2000. New technologies and old teachings: Problems and possibilities with ECD in the 21st century. Paper presented at Early Childhood World Forum, Singapore.

Pence, A.R., and J. Ball. 1999. Two sides of an eagle's feather: Co-constructing ECCD training curricula in university partnerships with Canadian First Nations communities. In *Theory, policy and practice in early childhood services,* ed. H. Penn, 36-47. Buckingham, UK: Open University Press.

Pence, A.R., V. Kuehne, M. Greenwood, and M.R. Opekokew. 1993. Generative curriculum: A model of university and First Nations cooperative post-secondary education. *International Journal of Educational Development* 13 (4): 339-49.

Pence, A.R., and M. McCallum. 1994. Developing cross-cultural partnerships: Implications for child care quality, research, and practice. In *Valuing quality in early childhood services: New approaches to defining quality,* ed. P. Moss and A.R. Pence, 108-22. New York: Teachers College Press.

Penn, H. 1997. *Comparing nurseries: Staff and children in Italy, Spain and the UK.* London: Paul Chapman.

–. 2005. *Understanding early childhood: Issues and controversies.* Maidenhead, UK: Open University Press.

Penn, H., and M. Molteno. 1997. Sustainability in early childhood development projects. UNICEF discussion paper. Florence: Innocenti Centre.

Riggan, R., and A. Kemble. 1994. The Cowichan Tribes early childhood education child and youth care career ladder project. Unpublished report, Malaspina University-College, Duncan Campus, British Columbia.

Robertson, D.L. 1996. Facilitating transformative learning: Attending to the dynamics of the educational helping relationship. *Adult Education Quarterly* 47 (1): 41-53.

Rogoff, B. 1994. Developing understanding of the idea of communities of learners. *Mind, Culture, and Activity* 1 (4): 209-29.

–. 2003. *The cultural nature of human development.* New York: Oxford University Press.

Romanow, R.J. 2002. *Building on values: The future of health care in Canada.* Ottawa: Commission on the Future of Health Care in Canada.

Rosenthal, M.K. 2003. Quality in early childhood education and care: A cultural context. *European Early Childhood Education Research Journal* 11 (2): 101-16.

Ross, R. 1992. *Dancing with a ghost: Exploring Indian reality.* Markham, ON: Reed Books.

Royal Commission on Aboriginal Peoples. 1996. *Report of the Royal Commission on Aboriginal Peoples.* Ottawa: Government of Canada.

Schwandt, T.A. 1996. Farewell to criteriology. *Qualitative Inquiry* 3 (1): 58-72.

Shiva, V. 1997. Western science and its destruction of local knowledge. In *The post-development reader,* ed. M. Rahnema and V. Bawtree, 161-67. London: Zed Books.

Smith, C., H. Burke, and G.K. Ward. 2000. Globalisation and Indigenous peoples: Threat or empowerment? In *Indigenous cultures in an interconnected world,* ed. C. Smith and G.K. Ward, 1-26. Vancouver: UBC Press.

Smith, L.T. 1999. *Decolonizing methodologies: Research and Indigenous peoples.* London: Zed Books.

Sparks, B. 1998. The politics of culture and the struggle to get an education. *Adult Education Quarterly* 48 (4): 245-59.

Stahl, A. 1992. Personal and cultural factors interfering with the effective use of individual and group learning methods. *Journal of Educational Thought* 26 (1): 22-32.

Statistics Canada. 2001a. *Aboriginal peoples survey.* Ottawa: Government of Canada.

–. 2001b. *Census of the population.* Ottawa: Government of Canada.

–. 2003. 2001 census: Analysis series. *Aboriginal peoples of Canada: A demographic profile.* Ottawa: Government of Canada.

Steffe, L., and J. Gale, eds. 1995. *Constructivism in education*. Mahwah, NJ: Lawrence Erlbaum.

Steinhauer, N. 1998. Higher education and Native students. *Canadian Social Studies* 32 (4): 115.

Swadener, B.B. 2000. "At risk" or "at promise"? From deficit constructions of the "other childhood" to possibilities for authentic alliances with children and families. In *The politics of early childhood education*, ed. L.D. Soto, 117-34. New York: P. Lang.

Swadener, B.B., and S. Kessler, eds. 1991. Reconceptualizing early childhood education. Special issue. *Early Education and Development* 2 (2).

Taylor, D.M., M.B. Crago, and L. McAlpine. 1993. Education in Aboriginal communities: Dilemmas around empowerment. *Canadian Journal of Native Education* 20: 176-83.

–. 2001. Toward full empowerment in Native education: Unanticipated challenges. *Canadian Journal of Native Studies* 21 (1): 45-56.

Taylor, E.W. 1994. Intercultural competency: A transformative learning process. *Adult Education Quarterly* 44 (3): 154-74.

Tobin, J., D. Wu, and D. Davidson. 1989. *Preschool in three cultures: Japan, China and the United States*. New Haven, CT: Yale University Press.

Toulmin, S. 1990. *Cosmopolis: The hidden agenda of modernity*. Chicago: University of Chicago Press.

Valsiner, J., and J. Litvinovic. 1996. Processes of generalization in parental reasoning. In *Parents' cultural belief systems: Their origins, expressions and consequences*, ed. S. Harkness and C. Super, 56-81. New York: Guilford Press.

Waldram, J.B. 2004. *Revenge of the Windigo: The construction of the mind and mental health of North American Aboriginal peoples*. Toronto: University of Toronto Press.

White, J.P., and P. Maxim. 2003. *Aboriginal conditions: The research foundations of public policy*. Vancouver: UBC Press.

White, J.P., P. Maxim, and D. Beavon. 2004. *Aboriginal policy research: Setting the agenda for change*. 2 vols. Toronto: Thompson Educational Publishing.

Whyte, K. 1982. The development of curricula/programs for Indian and Métis people. *Canadian Journal of Native Education* 9 (2): 121-29.

Wilson, P. 1994. The professor/student relationship: Key factors in minority student performance and achievement. *Canadian Journal of Native Studies* 14 (2): 305-17.

Woodhead, M. 1996. *In search of the rainbow: Pathways to quality in large-scale programmes for disadvantaged children*. The Hague: Bernard van Leer Foundation.

Woodhead, M., D. Faulkner, and K. Littleton, eds. 1998. *Cultural worlds of early childhood*. London: Routledge.

Index

Printed and bound in Canada by Friesens

Set in Giovanni Book and Garamond Condensed by Artegraphica Design Co. Ltd.

Copy editor: Judy Phillips

Proofreader: Sarah Munro

Indexer: Leslie Prpich

Cartographer: Eric Leinberger